FM29

THE LIMITS OF PERFORMANCE
IN THE FRENCH ROMANTIC THEATRE

Copyright © Susan McCready 2007

The right of Susan McCready to be identified as the author of this work has been asserted by her in accordance with the Copyright, Designs and Patents Act 1988.

Published by Manchester University Press
Oxford Road, Manchester M13 9NR, UK
and Room 400, 175 Fifth Avenue, New York, NY 10010, USA
www.manchesteruniversitypress.co.uk

Distributed in the United States exclusively by
Palgrave Macmillan, 175 Fifth Avenue,
New York, NY 10010, USA

Distributed in Canada exclusively by
UBC Press, University of British Columbia, 2029 West Mall,
Vancouver, BC, Canada V6T 1Z2

British Library Cataloguing-in-Publication Data is available

Library of Congress Cataloging-in-Publication Data is available

ISBN 978 0 7190 8191 0 paperback

First published by Durham Modern Languages Series 2007

This paperback edition published 2014

The publisher has no responsibility for the persistence or accuracy of URLs for any external or third-party internet websites referred to in this book, and does not guarantee that any content on such websites is, or will remain, accurate or appropriate.

Printed by Lightning Source

THE LIMITS OF PERFORMANCE IN THE FRENCH ROMANTIC THEATRE

By

Susan McCready

Durham Modern Languages Series 2007

Contents

Acknowledgements	vi
Introduction	1
Chapter I: Proof	15
Chapter II: Resistance	51
Chapter III: Sacrifice	81
Conclusion	127
Bibliography	131

For my students

Acknowledgements

I wish to thank the following for their financial support of this project: the University of South Alabama, Department of Foreign Languages and Literatures; the University of South Alabama, College of Arts and Sciences; the University of Pennsylvania, Department of Romance Languages; the Andrew W. Mellon Foundation; and the Centre International des Édutiants et Stagiares. In addition to their generous financial support, the members of the College of Arts and Sciences of the University of South Alabama and, most especially, my colleagues in the Department of Foreign Languages and Literatures, have been an unending font of moral and intellectual support, for which I will always be grateful. My two department chairs, Bernard Quinn and Calvin Jones, who have both been excellent mentor and sources of encouragement, deserve particular thanks.

Many other individuals also contributed to the development of this book from what now seems like its prehistoric incarnation as a dissertation on the theatre of Alfred de Musset to its present form. First and foremost, I must thank my dissertation advisor, Lucienne Frappier-Mazur, whose exacting standards helped me to achieve better work than I thought myself capable of. My original dissertation committee also included the late Charles Bernheimer and the late Frank Paul Bowman, both of whom are sorely missed. Jean-Marie Roulin stepped in at the last minute to read the dissertation after Charles Bernheimer's death, demonstrating the kind of intellectual generosity to who we in the humanities should all aspire.

Through its various forms, many colleagues, past and present, have read the manuscript and provided valuable insights. I am particularly grateful to Kristina Busse, Anne Duncan, Nancy Grey, Pratima Prasad, Daniel Price and Geri Smith.

I would never have completed this project without the love and patience of my family, especially by husband, Julien Lartigue. Thank you.

Finally my thanks to the staff of the Durham Modern Languages Series, Durham University, especially to Janet Starkey, for transforming the manuscript into my very first real book.

Introduction

We learn from the Bible that belief has trouble sustaining itself. The Israelites must repeatedly be brought back into obedience to Yahweh through various displays of God's power: in plagues, in defeats and in victories, variously interpreted by believers as signs of God's pleasure or displeasure. The Israelites must in turn act out their obedience to God, marking their bodies in circumcision, performing rituals of purification and belonging. Throughout the Bible, these physical acts of man and God are the negotiating principle between abstract belief and lived reality and in this way become a basic element of the structure of belief in our culture.

The structural kinship between the performance of religious ritual and theatrical performance has long been understood, for the origins of our western theatrical traditions lie precisely with religion, in the ritual sacrifice. There, the victim's body stood as substantiating proof of the realness of an abstract value (the existence of God). In theatre, the bodies of other victims, of Agamemnon and Hamlet and Lorenzaccio, substantiate in the concrete space of the stage values held or questioned both by authors and their audiences. In this way, the theatrical performance inherits not only its structure but also its function from the religious rituals at its source. But since the relationship between abstract idea and concrete manifestation — a relationship negotiated by the intermediary principle of performance — is neither simple, nor direct, nor stable, doubts resurface and the performance ritual must be repeated to keep them at bay.

Doubts about marital fidelity, for example, are ubiquitous in plays of all periods and genres, and we might argue that they simply reflect cultural or even biological anxieties about sexual fidelity, which so much of human culture attempts to guarantee. I contend however that anxieties about sexual fidelity acted out in the theatre exemplify deeper cultural anxieties about fidelity in the larger sense, and moreover, that the theatrical performance is structured to allay these anxieties. In comedy, a doubt about fidelity enters the supposedly stable system of marriage; then, over the course of the play, disguises are worn and letters are intercepted and the doubt is eventually exorcised as some physical evidence surfaces to reunite the couple. Finally, as in Alfred de Musset's *Caprice*, which is discussed in Chapter One, the happy couple stands for the audience as physical evidence of the value of fidelity. Treated in a tragic mode, marital infidelity may leave us instead with dead bodies, as in Alfred de Vigny's *Chatterton*, also treated in Chapter One. Here, the platonic adultery of Kitty Bell and the eponymous hero is consummated only in their shared death; the bodies of the lovers stand, then, as proof of a higher love, unsullied by the laws of man.

When I speak about anxieties about fidelity 'in the larger sense', I am accepting as given the post-structuralist contention that values and meanings are not inherent to signs, ideas or objects, but are referential. Values, always contingent and eligible for revision, are derived in reference to other values, which are, of course, contingent on other values and so on. The system is circular, with everything depending on something else for validation, and since there is nothing outside of the system, there is no possibility of establishing a grounded or original meaning or value. The suspicion that there is no external, verifiable value at the base of our systems of language, culture, and exchange creates an anxiety that leads us on a never-ending quest to find a way to ground the system, a way to guarantee the fidelity of signs.

The way we ground an abstract concept is to give it physical form. The flag represents the Nation; the cross represents Jesus (himself a physical form of the invisible Yahweh); the wedding ring represents sexual fidelity. But since the relationship is not based on an immutable law of physics, but only on an evolving cultural agreement, the sign will never be enough to allay once and for all our doubts about the truth or value of these ideas. Performances (ritual, theatrical, athletic and military) fulfil the same function as symbols, but in a more dynamic way. The military performance is an acting-out of a group's abstract claims to superiority over the enemy through which they resolve, for a time, their self-doubt by creating physical evidence of their superiority in the bodies of the dead and wounded on the other side. Likewise, in its staging of conflicts of values in the concrete space of the stage, the theatrical performance gives body to the abstract ideas announced in the dramatic text. Still, the meaning of any performance is no more fixed than the meaning of a symbol, and so performances must be repeated again and again to allay recurring doubts. What this means for culture is that it exists in a perpetual state of doubt, of crisis. Julia Przybos has argued in her excellent reading of French melodrama as Durkheimien ritual that a resurgence of melodrama at any given historical moment usually accompanies a cultural crisis, and that the purpose of melodrama is to enact a ritual of purification through which the community can face the crisis.[1] While I generally agree with her reading, that melodrama has a ritual function, it seems to me that Pryzbos defines crisis too narrowly to include only political, economic or social crises. There is a deeper crisis that underlies culture itself to which different kinds of performance are constantly responding. Since the central questions that culture tries to answer, questions about identity and values, can be answered only in terms that are constantly in flux, the answers have to be renegotiated all the time. Performances (religious, theatrical, military) are a way to reconfirm our definitions of, for example, the value of fidelity or honour or what it means to belong to one culture and not another. Performance temporarily obscures the fluidity of values by presenting us with something materially solid to set down next to the abstract idea. The wedding ring for the wedding vow; the sacrificial victim for the power of God; the body of Phèdre for the dangers of sexuality. We escape temporarily the infinite cycle of referentiality as for a time there is physical proof of the abstract concept in which we need to believe for our particular society to survive.

While within the play the text negotiates the shaky ground of values, the performance itself is structured to do the same thing. Western theatre is built upon the acting out of the abstract content of a text in a concrete stage space. The spectator must negotiate between the space of the stage, to which he or she is denied access by convention, and the world outside the theatre where he or she lives. Moreover, the spectator must navigate between the time of the performance (which is always synchronous with his or her own present tense) and the abstract time of the play (which may

[1] Julia Przybos, 'Melodrama as Social Ritual', *Theatre and Society in French Literature*, French Literature Series, vol. 25 (Columbia: University of South Carolina, 1988), 86–94.

represent past, present or future, morning, afternoon or evening, an hour, a week or a moment). In reaction to a world where everything is contingent and nothing stands solidly outside of made culture as its guarantor, the staged performance sets up an inside (the stage) and an outside (the hall). It is on the border between these two spaces that the theatre fulfils its most sacred function: the making of meaning.

This study will attempt to map out that border using a specific theatrical movement as a case in point. The French Romantics were fascinated by the theatre and by theatrical performance. In their lives, as in their novels, poems and plays, the theatre and the performer held a place of honour. In fact, all of the major writers of the nineteenth century – from Balzac to Zola – attempted (with varying degrees of success) to write for the theatre. I have chosen to focus narrowly on thirteen self-consciously theatrical works by four authors from the 1830s: Alfred de Vigny (1797–1863), Alexandre Dumas, *père* (1802–1870), Victor Hugo (1802–1885) and Alfred de Musset (1810–1857). As the characters in these plays don disguises, play roles and stage plays-within-the-play to arrive at their ends, we can chart out the possible trajectories of performance and begin to make an argument about how performance responds to the deeper anxieties informing Romantic theatre and nineteenth-century culture.

The interdisciplinary field of performance theory has developed multiple approaches to address the study of theatre (anthropological, phenomenological, and semiological) and I intend to draw on several of them for the present study. Much of the work in performance theory has dealt, logically, with arriving at a definition of the term 'performance', and before I go any further, I should say that I am generally using the word as anthropologist / performance theorist Richard Schechner defines it. Schechner has argued for a broad definition of the term 'performance', within the field of performance studies, stating,

> Performance is an inclusive term. Theatre is only one mode on a continuum that reaches from the ritualisations of animals (including humans) through performances in everyday life... through to play, sports, theatre, dance, ceremonies, rites and performances of great magnitude.[2]

[2] Richard Schechner, *Performance Theory* (New York and London: Routledge,

Anthropologists, including Schechner, Victor Turner and others, have sought to outline the basic structures of ritual performance and to find continuities between the ritual and performance structures common to all cultures, for as Schechner says, 'The phenomena, called either / all "drama", "theatre", "performance" occur among all the world's peoples and date back as far as historians archaeologists and anthropologists can go.'[3]

Victor Turner's description of the 'social drama', by which cultural norms are breached and then order (usually) restored lays the groundwork for a discussion of the negotiation of values through performance. He outlines a four-step process in which 1) breach occurs, as social norms are transgressed; 2) crisis ensues, as norms are questioned and hidden rifts revealed; 3) redressive action (religious or judicial) takes place; and 4) order is restored or 4b) the breach is recognised as definitive.[4] Step 3 is the ritual stage, the in-between state where the result is yet to be decided. He states:

> All these 'third-phase' ... ritual processes contain within themselves what I have in several writings called a liminal phase, which provides a stage (and I use this term advisedly when thinking about theatre) for unique structures of experience... which I have elsewhere described as liminal. The limen, or threshold, a term I took from van Gennep's second of three stages in rites of passage is a no-man's-land betwixt-and-between the structural past and the structural future.[5]

As we continue our discussion of the 'limits' of performance, Turner's limen, describing the stage as an intermediate zone between before and after where culture works itself out, will be always in the background. Although his ideas have rarely been applied to performance theory, Georges Bataille's[6] diverse writings (some of which would fall into the cate-

---

1988), xiii.
[3] Ibid., 68.
[4] Victor Turner, 'Are there universals of performance in myth, ritual and drama?' in *By Means of Performance*, Richard Schechner and Willa Appel (eds) (Cambridge: Cambridge University Press, 1990), 8–18.
[5] Ibid., 11.
[6] A recent doctoral thesis on German expressionist theatre by Jeffrey Salyer, 'The

gory of 'anthropological', though he was not a trained anthropologist) also inform my approach and particularly my understanding of the border space that performance occupies. Bataille's concepts of expenditure, discussed in Chapter One and the *expérience des limites*, discussed at length in Chapter Two, will in particular help us to explore the role of (indeed, the constitution of) the individual and the community in performance. Although the larger question of how performance functions in culture interests me, I am no anthropologist, and I will draw on other sources both from within the field of performance studies and from outside the field as I endeavour to explore the structure and purpose of performance in the French Romantic theatre in the rest of this volume. Semiology in particular is relevant, because as Patrice Pavis states,

> Semiology does not concern itself with locating meaning ... but with the mode of production of that meaning throughout the theatrical process, beginning with the director's reading of the script through to the interpreting task of the spectator.[7]

As one of the only performance theorists to have published extensively on the French Romantic theatre, semiologist Anne Ubersfeld holds a privileged place in the present study as well. In fact, her monograph on Victor Hugo is a cornerstone of my discussion of his work in Chapter Two.

In her theoretical work, Ubersfeld has demonstrated the referential structure of theatre, which I outlined above. According to Ubersfeld, the spectator of a theatrical performance does not simply 'believe in' the reality of what is enacted on stage, but performs a psychological negotiation (which she calls 'dénégation') to discern the referential relationship of two real spaces, that of the concrete ('real') space of the stage and that of quotidian reality, 'there where his action is exercised, there where he is not a spectator'.[8] The spectator understands that the stage space and the

---

Expressionist Stage in Light of Bataillian Expenditure', presented at the University of Washington in 1999, is the only book-length application of Bataille's concepts to performance theory to date.

[7] Patrice Pavis, *Languages of the Stage* (New York: Performing Arts Journal Publications, 1982), 13.

[8] Anne Ubersfeld, 'Notes sur la dénégation théâtrale', in *La Relation théâtrale*, Régis Durand (ed.) (Lille: Presses Universitaires de Lille, 1980) 11, my transla-

actions that take place there are fictions, but fictions — made things — that find their referents in the world where he lives. Although at odds with semiologists on many points, phenomenologist Bert O. States similarly rejects the idea of a simply representational relationship between stage and world. He contends, 'The actor takes us into a world within the world itself. At bottom, it is not a matter of the illusory, the mimetic, or the representational, but of a certain kind of actual, of having something before one's vision – and in the theatre one's hearing – to which we join our being.'[9] Likewise, performance theorist Richard Bauman argues that, 'all performance involves a consciousness of doubleness, through which the actual execution of an action is placed in *mental comparison* with a potential, an ideal, or a remembered original model of that action'.[10] While I disagree with the notion that there can be an 'original model' for any action,[11] what strikes me with Bauman as with both States and Ubersfeld, is that for all of these theorists, the spectator is not passively experiencing the theatrical performance, but participating in the negotiation of the relationship between the stage world and his or her own world. It is this relationship that I will attempt to disentangle in what follows.

Perhaps surprisingly, the theorist to whom I will most often refer, Elaine Scarry, is not a performance theorist, nor is her work often cited in the vast literature on performance theory.[12] Still, Elaine Scarry's work provides a clear structure for understanding the relationship between the abstract text and the concrete stage, and for exploring the relationship between the abstract values announced in the play and the material effects

tion.
[9] Bert O. States, *Great Reckonings in Little Rooms: on the phenomenology of Theater* (Berkeley: University of California Press, 1985), 46.
[10] Cited by Marvin Carlson, *Performance: A critical introduction* (London and New York: Routledge, 1996), 6.
[11] In fact, the French word for performance is 'représentation', which implies a structurally inherent repetition, a re-presentation.
[12] The only use of Scarry (besides my own) in performance theory literature I have so far located is Jeanie Forte's, 'Focus on the Body: Pain Praxis, and Pleasure in Feminist Performance', in *Critical Theory and Performance*, Janelle G. Reinelt, and Joseph R. Roach (eds) (Ann Arbor: University of Michigan Press, 1992), 248–62.

of those values in culture. She argues in her book *The Body in Pain: the making and unmaking of the world* that cultures or individuals seek to embody their abstract values in physical bodies and often in physical pain. Thus the pretensions of a nation to moral or physical superiority find their anchor, their 'analogical verification' to use Scarry's term, in the wounded and dead bodies of the soldiers on the battlefield. Likewise, the God of the Israelites proves his own reality not by showing his body (for he has no body), but by marking the bodies of those who believe in him (in circumcision) and those who refuse him (in plagues, for example). What we are getting at when we try to understand how the physical stage space endows otherwise abstract fictions with meaning, is the very structure of belief, the process by which meaning is produced.

The ritual sacrifice united the community as witnesses to the power of God, of law, of the unembodied values without which there can be no community. The community thus constitutes itself in the (re)-enactment of its own power on the body of the victim. The victim stands perhaps for the worst of the community, the outcast or the diseased, and the victim's removal, so the story goes, insures that the community can live on. Perhaps, on the other hand, the victim is the best the community has to offer and the sacrifice of that dear member sanctifies the whole community and binds them together in loss, in grief and in powerlessness in the face of a jealous god. In either case there are two steps: the body is opened and then a story is told. We no longer open bodies on altars, but we still need bodies to tell our stories. The bodies of Lorenzo and Hernani are present to us on stage and their story thus retold constitutes the spectators as more than individual witnesses but as a community of interpreters, who understand the actions on stage to have meaning beyond the formal elements of theatre.[13]

The principle of substitution, which is central to the ritual sacrifice, is an underlying structure of drama, where the actor stands in for the character and the stage stands in for the world. Within the theatrical performance, too, many devices can be read through the idea of substitution. The comic device of *quiproquo*, for example, etymologically 'something for

---

[13] See Chapter Three for a more complete treatment of these theoretical problems.

something', is a substitution of one word or idea for another, a comic misunderstanding that results from a failure to define terms and agree on the meanings of certain words, usually pronouns. Masks, be they in either the tragic or the comic mode, involve the substitution of a true face for a false one, and may represent the *mise en abyme* of the actor's enterprise. In traditional comedies, it is the business of the play to eliminate the indeterminacy occasioned by these devices through performances that arrive at the truth. The unmasking of the villain at the end of a melodrama serves the same function, clarifying the action of the play and uniting both the surviving characters and the audience in their understanding of the events they have witnessed. Of course, this is not always the resolution and the play can end with no understanding at all and the values still in flux. Our exploration of French Romantic theatre will focus in part on these structures and their results in an attempt to show how performance can both occasion and dispel doubt.

If, as I have argued, deep societal anxieties about the nature of values are indeed being enacted in theatre, then we should not proceed without situating the theatre we are studying within its socio-historical context. The Restoration era and the July Monarchy (1815–1848) established a relative calm after the tumultuous Revolution of 1789, the Terror, the rise of Napoleon and his final defeat at Waterloo. Still, it was an uneasy period, marked by economic difficulties and by the political instability that eventually led to the revolution of 1830, the abdication of Charles X and the ascension of Louis-Philippe, the Bourgeois King. The Enlightenment ideal of the social contract had taken root and the people refused to tolerate Charles X's autocratic attempts to suppress the Charter. At the same time, an artistic movement aimed at loosening the restrictive rules that defined official French theatre was taking shape and would lead to the other revolution of 1830, as Victor Hugo's Romantic drama *Hernani* triumphed at the Comédie Française. This period was characterised by self-conscious reflections on the nature of government and the social contract and parallel reflections about the nature of theatre and the idea of spectacle. It is not coincidental that Victor Hugo's alliance shifted from the monarchy to the republican left just as his *Hernani* became the centre of the most heated literary debate of the century.

The Revolution of 1789 had opened up the theatre scene in France enormously, as the decree of January 1791 had authorised 'tout citoyen à élever un théâtre public et à y faire représenter des pièces de tous les genres'.[14] Censorship, which since 1701 had required that every play be read and approved before its performance, was also abolished.[15] Napoleon restored a strict control of theatres and the role of the censor in a series of decrees in 1806–1807 and the Restoration continued the practice. Censorship was abolished again in 1830 and reinstated again in 1850,[16] but the enormous popularity of the private 'boulevard' theatres, located on some of the major thoroughfares of Paris, remained constant throughout these many political and administrative changes. Unconcerned with issues of repertoire and the dignity of French cultural heritage, they were giving people what they wanted: the melodrama and the Romantic *drame*. So while there was no lack of space in which the Romantics could have their work performed — indeed many of the best Romantic plays premiered 'on the boulevard' — they yet craved the recognition that only the Comédie Française, whose official mandate was to preserve the classical repertoire, could provide.

Partisans of the Romantic theatre championed experimentation with dramatic form. They wanted to release the theatre from the shackles of the unities (of time and place — they accept the unity of action) which, inspired by Aristotle, had developed into doctrine over the course of the seventeenth century in France. Moreover, the Romantics sought to infuse modern history into the theatre, abandoning the old stories of Greek and Roman history and mythology for more contemporary subjects. The very definition of 'theatre' was at stake in a battle between pamphleteers, for example, Stendhal's *Racine et Shakespeare* (1822–1825) and prefaces, notably Hugo's *Préface de Cromwell* (1827), that reached a fever pitch on the opening night of Hugo's *Hernani*. The central aesthetic question

[14] Cited in Anne Ubersfeld, *Le Drame Romantique* (Paris: Belin, 1993), 85.
[15] Censorship existed prior to 1701, of course, but was performed in an *ad hoc* and (as in the case of Molière) often *ad hominem* manner.
[16] For a complete discussion of censorship during this era see Odile Krakovitch, 'Les Romantiques et la censure au théâtre', *Revue d'Histoire du Théâtre*, 36: 1 (January–March 1984), 56–68.

that informed the debates was whether or not the rules of *tragédie classique* were immutable laws of the theatre or simply conventions whose time had passed. The eighteenth century had already witnessed great developments in theatrical form, with Voltaire's stage reforms, Diderot's *drame bourgeois* and the rise of the melodrama; but not until the Romantic debates did partisans of dramatic reform demand the recognition and official sanction of seeing the *drame* performed at the Comédie Française. Much of the debate centred on *vraisemblance*, the verisimilitude of the plays espousing the new Romantic doctrines. The unities of time and space, argued the 'classiques', allow the theatrical illusion to exist: how can you expect the spectator to believe that the space that in the first act was Venice is now Cyprus? How can you expect the spectator to understand or believe that days or weeks have passed when he knows he has been in the theatre only three hours? The Romantics, Germaine de Staël, Benjamin Constant and Stendhal leading the way, respond that what is unbelievable is that a king and a servant should both speak in perfect and indistinguishable alexandrine verse. They respond that what is preposterous is that French theatre should spin its wheels indefinitely, refusing all outside influence, and growing ever more threadbare. Stendhal, appealing to the commercial interests that would finally win the day, sums up:

> Le romanticisme [sic] est l'art de présenter aux peuples les œuvres littéraires qui, dans l'état actuel de leurs habitudes et de leurs croyances, sont susceptibles de leur donner le plus de plaisir possible. Le classicisme, au contraire, leur présente la littérature qui donnait le plus grand plaisir à leurs arrière-grand-pères.[17]

Unconvinced as to the aesthetic question, but suffering financially despite government subsidy, the Comédie Française finally could not resist the money to be made by the *drame*.[18] In 1829, they somewhat reluctantly performed Alexandre Dumas' *Henri III et sa cour* and Alfred de Vigny's

---

[17] Stendhal, *Racine et Shakespeare* (Paris: Garnier-Flammarion, 1970), 71.
[18] Ironically enough, many nineteenth-century authors loudly decried the commercialisation (which they equated with the debasement) of art. See Musset's *André del Sarto* (1832), for example. Yet, finally, only the commercial appeal of Romantic drama would open the doors to the official theatres.

adaptation of *Othello, Le More de Venise*, but it was not until what become known as the Bataille d'*Hernani* in February of 1830 that the Comédie Française capitulated. They would continue to perform the repertory works of the masters, but after 1830 many of the important Romantic works (notably Vigny's *Chatterton* in 1835) premiered there or at the other state subsidised theatre, the Odéon.[19]

Despite this victory, the first half of the nineteenth century in France represents a time of disillusion and disappointment for the writers coming of age. While the Romantics of the generation of 1830 had not for the most part experienced the 1789 Revolution, they were still feeling the effects of the political and social upheavals that began before 1789 with the Enlightenment philosophers. In considering the pre-history of this era (the Ancien Régime, the Revolution, Napoleon) we are less concerned with the specific historic events than with the resonance that events and ideas had with the writers of our period. Alfred de Musset's account of the times and of the famous *mal du siècle* afflicting his generation appears in the second chapter of his 1836 autobiographical novel *La Confession d'un enfant du siècle*. The Ancien Régime has gone, taking with it the faith in the divine right of kings; the Revolution of 1789, which was supposed to guarantee the Rights of Man and Citizen, has failed; even Napoleon, who promised and delivered an Empire, is finally revealed to be only a man. 'Alors s'assit sur un monde en ruines une jeunesse soucieuse,'[20] Musset writes.

France is ruled once again by a monarch, but one who derives his power not from divine right, but from the Charter. The absolutes on which the monarchy (and the whole system of belief) had been based are revealed to have been illusory, and are replaced only by endless rounds of debate and rhetoric. Musset's generation is a sea amidst the wreckage of the old order; their faith is gone, but their future is yet to be determined. 'Voilà,' he writes, 'dans quel chaos il fallut choisir alors; voilà ce qui se présentait à des enfants pleins de force et d'audace, fils de l'Empire et petits-fils de la Révolution.'[21] Here, as elsewhere in French Romanticism,

---

[19] *Hernani* and the scandal surrounding it are discussed in Chapter Two.
[20] Alfred de Musset, *Œuvres complètes en prose* (Paris: Gallimard 1951), 83.
[21] Ibid., 85.

we see the young generation at the mercy of contradictory forces: the nostalgia for what is lost and the hope or fear of what is to come. Musset concludes the chapter with an apostrophe to the people of future generations who will have passed this difficult moment of indeterminacy. He implores them:

> pensez à nous qui n'y serons plus; dites-vous que nous avons acheté bien cher le repos dont vous jouirez; plaignez-nous plus que tous vos pères; car nous avons beaucoup des maux qui les rendaient dignes de plainte, et nous avons perdu ce qui les consolait.[22]

It is precisely this loss of faith, the instability it occasions, and the attempts to arrive at some new way of believing that we will see enacted again and again in the Romantic theatre and in Musset's theatre in particular.

The Romantic theatre has a few characteristic obsessions, some of which it inherits from melodrama or the *drame bourgeois,* others of which are innovations that the Romantics introduce to the French stage. Disguises and masks are certainly not new to the theatre, but they become almost omnipresent in Romantic theatre where they serve as props in an investigation of the nature of the individual. Characters in disguise escape their prescribed place in society and discover worlds that would be otherwise out of their reach. Moreover, a concern with father figures and naming characterises the Romantic hero, who is both drawn to the past and blocked by the patriarchal order from access in his own name to the stage of history. In these obsessions we can see a reflection of the Revolution and of the fall of Napoleon. The execution of Louis XVI and the exile of Napoleon have tremendous resonance in French literature throughout the century, as writers attempt to come to terms with the deaths of these two symbolic fathers.

I want to be perfectly clear that although I hope the present study will contribute to a better understanding of the Romantic theatre and of France in the 1830s, it is not intended as a socio-historical study of the early nineteenth century in France as seen through its theatre. It is rather a

---

[22] Ibid., 95.

study of the structures of theatre and of performance which uses French Romantic theatre as its case in point, aimed at a better understanding of how performance works in the complex negotiation of values both on the stage and in our world: how make-believe makes us believe. I am not arguing that the cultural or historical context in which Romantic theatre arose is irrelevant; nor that history and culture do not produce unique crises to which a historically or culturally specific ritual or art responds: only that behind the particular questions or doubts or crises, there lies an open question common to culture. It is that open question, the basic question about the relationship between visible and invisible, between object and idea, that ritual in its infinite variety attempts to answer.

Chapter I: Proof[1]

A young man is promised in marriage to a young woman. But before saying 'I do' he must prove to himself that she truly loves him and will be faithful to him. Disguises are worn; letters are intercepted; conversations overheard, but in the end, the lovers recognise each other's true, essential value and are united. This is a standard comic plot: some sort of conflict (a doubt about fidelity) is introduced into a once-stable system (an arranged marriage) and the conflict is resolved through 'negotiations', which, in the end, uphold the (slightly altered) *status quo*.[2] The traditional comic resolution eliminates a sometimes sinister indeterminacy, through a performance of stability — usually the promise of the marriage of the protagonists to the 'correct' partner. The young lovers in such traditional comedies are exemplary figures whose negotiations about fidelity or marriage can be read in general terms as meditations on the collectively imagined value of love, fidelity and marriage in society. The happy resolution of the conflict is a 'making real', to use Elaine Scarry's term, of these abstract values, which are now anchored for the audience in the theatrical performance and for the characters by some performance *within* the play.

Elaine Scarry shows in *The Body in Pain* how anxieties about indeterminacy, what she calls 'unanchored claims' — such as the claim of the realness of God — lead to the complex, collective psychological project of *analogical verification*, which consists of anchoring those claims in a

---

[1] The introduction and Part One of this chapter are revised from Susan McCready, 'Performing Stability: the problem of proof in Alfred de Musset's *Un Caprice* and *La Quenouille de Barbérine*', *Romance Notes*, 38: 1 (Fall 1997), 7–95.
[2] This is basically the plot of Marivaux's *L'Épreuve* and *Le Jeu de l'amour et du hasard*, among others, but it is not limited to comedy. It is also the plot of *A Winter's Tale* and Chaucer's 'Clerk's Tale' (which is Perrault's 'Griselidis') and with the minor variation of an unhappy ending (in which the value of the spouse is recognised too late) becomes the basic plot of *Othello*.

physical body and usually in physical pain.³ For example, according to Scarry, in the Old Testament, scenes of wounding are meant to substantiate, to 'make real' the existence of God; the marks on the bodies of the Israelites are to be read as 'proof' of the power of God, who has no body. This process is what 'grounds' the claim of God's realness, a claim on which an entire social order is based. We can also see this process at work in the theatre, in plays in which the conflict centres on the need to prove something — and in comedies it is often love or fidelity that is in question. The need for *physical* evidence — of love, of fidelity — drives the action of the play until the characters are satisfied, and in plays in the most traditional mode, satisfaction comes only with the happy marriage (performed or renewed) of the protagonists. At the same time, the play itself serves the function of analogical verification for its audience, whose unanchored claims about love and fidelity are embodied in the physical performance of the play.⁴

The six plays we will discuss in this chapter conform to this basic structure as characters rehearse a variety of strategies to arrive at some sort of proof. The strategies are the traditional comic devices such as secret, disguise (and recognition), and *dédoublement*, which at first heighten the indeterminacy — and the comic effect. In the end, however, the negotiation of values played out in these strategies reaches a resolution, a collective agreement about value(s) which (re)stabilises the system. Thus artificial indeterminacy (disguise, and so on) is a pretext to a performance of stability. A reading of two of Alfred de Musset's plays, *Un Caprice* and *La Quenouille de Barbérine*, will illustrate this process. Yet among even the lightest of comedies there are examples of a different kind of resolution, one in which *unresolved* indeterminacy in the systems of exchange (linguistic, financial, and social) puts into question the underlying values of a given social system (as might be found, for example,

---

[3]   Elaine Scarry, *The Body in Pain* (New York: Oxford University Press, 1985).
[4]   See Anne Ubersfeld, 'Notes sur la dénégation théâtrale', in *La Relation théâtrale*, Régis Durand (ed.) (Lille: Presses Universitaires de Lille, 1980), where, as I mentioned in the introduction to the present volume, she explores the referential relationship of *two* real spaces negotiated by the spectator, that of the concrete ('real') space of the stage and that of quotidian reality.

in marriage). Alfred de Vigny's *Quitte pour la peur* and Alexandre Dumas' *Kean* will serve as examples of this more open-ended resolution. If the comedy leaves open the possibility of negotiations within the system, the *drame* often closes all options down. As we will see in a reading of Vigny's *Chatterton* and Dumas' *Antony*, the *drame* presents a more extreme position in which the system is rejected entirely. The heroes of these plays try to find a way *not* to perform, a way for their bodies *not* to have meaning in what they perceive as a corrupt and degraded society. Their failure will reveal an essential breach between the individual and his society, as in death they are reintegrated into a system of meaning they refused in life.

In his *Confession d'un enfant du siècle*, Musset as social critic suffers precisely from his 'contemporary indeterminacy', a malaise, which according to him is endemic to his rudderless generation as it drifts between the past and the future. He describes the situation of the French youth in the 1830s thus:

> derrière eux un passé à jamais détruit, s'agitant encore sur ses ruines, avec tous les fossiles des siècles d'absolutisme; devant eux l'aurore d'un immense horizon, les premières clartés de l'avenir; et entre ces deux mondes... quelque chose de semblable à l'Océan qui sépare le vieux continent de la jeune Amérique, je ne sais quoi de vague et de flottant, une mer houleuse et pleine de naufrages, traversée de temps en temps par quelque blanche voile lointaine ou par quelque navire soufflant une lourde vapeur; le siècle présent, en un mot, qui sépare le passé de l'avenir, qui n'est ni l'un ni l'autre et qui ressemble à tous deux à la fois, et où l'on ne sait à chaque pas qu'on fait, si l'on marche sur une semence ou sur un débris.[5]

The plays we will discuss in this chapter are all in some way meditations on this indeterminacy and attempts to establish new exchange values through which the individual and the society might become 'grounded' once more.

---

[5] Musset, *Œuvres complètes en prose* (Paris: Gallimard, 1951), 85.

Part One. Performing Stability: Musset's Un Caprice *and* La Quenouille de Barbérine

Thanks in part to his tumultuous affair with George Sand, Alfred de Musset (1810–1857) is better known in the United States as a romantic than for being a Romantic author. But in fact his theatrical œuvre represents the most important and the most durable example of French Romantic drama and is the only French Romantic theatre belonging to the standard performance repertoires of the major continental companies today. Still, during his lifetime, Musset's theatrical career was not without frustrations. The première on 1 December 1830 of *La Nuit Vénitienne*, a diaphanous comedy in three scenes, was an utter disaster. Early in the performance, the lead actress Mlle Bérenger leaned against a freshly-painted balustrade and had to spend the rest of the show with green paint streaks marking her white dress; the audience howled. The play's mixture of passion and light comedy was disconcerting: the audience booed. The style of the play was 'moitié inintelligible et moitié ridicule', the critics railed.[6] Bitterly disappointed, young Musset swore off writing for the stage.

Musset continued to write plays, but none was produced until 1847 when *Un Caprice*, published in *La Revue des Deux Mondes* in 1837, brought Musset the theatrical success that had eluded him seventeen years before. From 1847 on, several of Musset's works were produced, some in 'scenic versions', which eliminated the scene changes and multiple sets called for in the original versions, written without concern for the difficulties of staging. Most Musset scholars agree that the failure of *La Nuit Vénitienne* was finally quite fortunate. In forsaking the physical stage, with its constraints, Musset's *Spectacle dans un fauteuil*, the title of his 1834 collection of plays, stretched the possibilities of the theatre. His work anticipates changes in the theatrical aesthetic, which made the performance of his major plays possible beginning in the 1920s and 30s. If he remains the most important playwright of the Romantic period it is

---

[6] From an anonymous review in *Le Commerce* (6 décembre, 1830), cited by Simon Jeune in the notes to Alfred de Musset, *Théâtre complet* (Paris: Gallimard, 1990), 862.

ironically thanks to the failure that freed him to explore the theatre in the abstract. Unlike Hugo and Dumas *père*, whose works appear dated and overdrawn, Musset's plays are more performed now than at any time during the author's life.

Musset as playwright has been compared to Shakespeare and Hoffman, to Schiller and Byron, to Walter Scott and Goethe. A late arrival on the Romantic stage, Musset distils the Romantic influences from home and abroad to create his own ironised version of the Romantic mythos. In the same year that he published *La Confession d'un enfant du siècle*, with its second chapter that reads like a Romantic manifesto, Musset produced a series of satirical articles entitled 'Lettres de Dupuis et Cotonet' in which two provincial readers attempting to define Romanticism conclude from a comparison of excerpts that 'le romantisme consiste à employer tous ces adjectifs, et non en autre chose'.[7] With wit and irony, Musset both takes the Romantic position and undermines it.

Chapter Three is devoted entirely to a discussion of Musset's four most important plays, plays of an indeterminate genre that earned him (posthumously) elegiac introductions like the one you have just read. Here, however, we will discuss two of the least problematic of Musset's plays, plays whose conventionality risks making the above introduction seem incongruous. While *Un Caprice* and *La Quenouille de Barbérine* embody certain concerns about performance, value and power, they do so within a system that presents the value of marriage and fidelity as a given. The fidelity of specific characters is put into question, but the value of fidelity is always agreed upon in the happy ending that reunites husband and wife. Certainly the better-known of these comedies is *Un Caprice*, a one-act play in eight scenes, whose performance at the Théâtre Français in 1847 marked the beginning of Musset's theatrical 'come-back' and which has been one of Musset's most performed plays ever since. *Un Caprice* is particularly illuminating as it opens with the proof of conjugal devotion (the purse Mathilde is making for her husband) and the proof of adultery (the *other*, 'counterfeit' purse accepted by the husband from another woman). The rest of the play is a series of manipulations that will 'set

---

[7] Musset, *Prose*, 852.

things right' again, negotiating an agreement about the essential value of fidelity. The happy endings of *Un Caprice* and *La Quenouille de Barbérine* illustrate that they are less about a general anxiety about systems of exchange than they are models of how to navigate them.

The opening scene of *Un Caprice* finds Mme de Chavigny (Mathilde) placing the finishing touches on a red purse she has made in secret as a surprise for her husband. Urged on by affection for her husband and her fear of losing him to another, Mathilde plans to offer the purse to her husband as a mark of her own fidelity. She has worked in secret, she explains, to avoid the appearance of a reproach: 'Cela aurait eu l'air de lui dire : 'Voyez comme je pense à vous' [...] tandis qu'en lui montrant mon petit travail fini, ce sera lui qui se dira que j'ai pensé à lui'.[8] She goes on to address an affectionate apostrophe to the purse in which it becomes clear that the real value of the purse is not in any intrinsic worth as an object, but in its offering. 'Pauvre petite! tu ne vaux pas grand-chose, on ne te vendrait pas deux louis. Comment se fait-il qu'il me semble triste de me séparer de toi!'[9] In fact, Mathilde has great difficulty in separating herself from the purse. Not only is she already clearly projecting her identity onto the purse, confounding herself psychologically with it,[10] but the act of offering the purse will be physically deferred and finally performed only through the mediation of Mme de Léry.

The first obstacle to offering the purse comes from Mathilde herself who has not finished it when her husband enters. He then proudly (one might say sadistically) displays another purse, a blue purse given to him as a gift. Mathilde's friend and confidante Mme de Léry then enters and immediately identifies the author of the blue purse as a Mme de Blainville, confirming Mathilde's suspicions. Mme de Léry's teasing remarks about the purse show a clear continuity with Mathilde's attitude toward her own purse. That is, here, a purse is not just a purse. 'On a mis sept ans

---

[8] Alfred de Musset, *Théâtre complet* (Paris: Gallimard, 1990), 422.
[9] Ibid.
[10] For example, after failing to present the purse to him, Mathilde is about to throw it on the fire and then stops herself and addressing the purse says: 'Mais qu'as-tu fait? [...] Il n'y a pas de ta faute; tu attendais, tu espérais aussi' (431). She is clearly projecting her own intentions onto her gift.

à la faire et vous jugez si pendant ce temps-là elle a changé de destination. Elle a appartenu en idée à trois personnes de ma connaissance. C'est un vrai trésor que vous avez là.'[11] While a specific item exchanged is not necessarily meaningful, the exchange itself always has meaning within the societal context.[12] In this case, the object is inscribed in the courtly tradition of love tokens, in which accepting a gift or wearing clothing in the lover's colour is part of a 'code' which signifies the lovers' constancy (or infidelity). Both Mme de Léry and Mathilde (and presumably Mme de Blainville) immediately understand this, but Chavigny refuses to accept the purse's 'meaning'. He makes much of Mathilde's nonsensical question on first seeing the purse: 'De quelle couleur est-elle?'[13] But, in fact, in the context of the courtly code, the colour signifies the purse's author and so to ask 'What colour is it?' is really to ask 'Who gave it to you?' Chavigny likewise sees, or claims to see, only nonsense in Mathilde's displeasure that he should display the purse in public, replying 'La montrer! Ne dirait-on pas que c'est un trophée?' Of course, that is precisely what it is: the purse represents his (imminent) conquest of Mme de Blainville and his denial of this fact makes his intentions all the more clear. When Mathilde begs Chavigny to give up the blue purse, the subtext is just as clear, but he again refuses, preferring to take everything literally in order to deny its signification.

It is Mme de Léry who, once apprised of the situation between the spouses, is able to turn Chavigny's refusal against him. She has Mathilde's purse presented to him anonymously, then teases him to guess its author. This time, it is she who a remains, at least in appearance, in the realm of the literal as Chavigny (convinced that the purse is a gift from Mme de Léry, herself) attempts to seduce her. In an inversion of his earlier scene with Mathilde, Chavigny begs to know who made the red purse, then gladly exchanges the blue one for it. The exchange made,

---

[11] Musset, *Théâtre*, 426.
[12] See also Marcel Mauss's 'Essai sur le don', in his *Sociologie et anthropologie* (Paris: Presses Universitaires Marcel Françaises, 1973), in which he analyses the gift as 'total social fact'. Of course, in this case, the choice of a purse is not arbitrary, but deeply significant, as we will see.
[13] Musset, *Théâtre*, 425.

Mme de Léry reveals that the red purse was made by Mathilde. With this moment of recognition everything falls back into place: Chavigny now understands the true value of Mathilde's love and plans to confess his faults to her and in so doing to restore conjugal felicity.

The obstacle to Chavigny's recognition of Mathilde's value is his own desire to have it both ways. In refusing to admit that his having accepted a purse from Mme de Blainville 'means' anything, he is able to keep both possibilities (fidelity or infidelity) 'in play'. He is able to do this because he himself is not engaged in the exchanges taking place. We have spoken of the purse as an 'arbitrary object' in the system of exchange, but in the realm of literature it is anything but arbitrary. As a metonymy for the woman who offers it, the purse has obvious sexual connotations and becomes the object of 'analogical verification' of which Elaine Scarry speaks. Not only, as we have seen, do the two purses 'make real' certain claims — Mathilde's stands for fidelity, while Mme de Blainville's stands for proof of infidelity — they illustrate the power imbalance inherent in the relationships of the characters. That is, they stand for the radical embodiment of the women as opposed to the un-embodied power of Chavigny who is able to refuse their signification as long as it is convenient because he is not himself embodied in the exchange. Scarry opposes the vulnerable, physical body to the powerful, un-embodied voice, and so it is no surprise if here the power exercised by the un-embodied Chavigny is discursive.

When in her confrontation with her husband in scene four, Mathilde falls on her knees to beg him to give up the blue purse (intending, unbeknownst to Chavigny, to replace it with the red one), the engagement of her body in this action exemplifies the degree to which she is already physically engaged in the exchange of the purses. Chavigny's reply and his immediate exit demonstrate his power; he is able to enforce his will discursively by naming Mathilde's action 'un enfantillage'[14] and physically by cutting off all discussion in leaving. In a way, Chavigny is already absent before his exit as he is not really 'in' the negotiation that Mathilde is attempting to operate. In scene viii, the analogous scene be-

[14] Ibid., 430.

tween Chavigny and Mme de Léry, the power imbalance is corrected. This time, Mathilde is physically absent from the stage (although metonymically figured in the presence of the red purse) and acting only as her proxy, Mme de Léry is not herself implicated in the exchange she successfully operates; that is, she is all voice. In contrast, Chavigny goes through a process of 'embodiment' over the course of the scene, as Mme de Léry (by withholding the name of the author of the red purse) is able to reverse the power dynamic of the earlier scene. Chavigny, himself, begs on bended knee to know the name of his admirer, as Mathilde had done earlier.

When Mme de Léry destroys the blue purse, however, the exchange is not complete, since Chavigny believes that Mme de Léry is the author of the red purse. Another substitution must be made before Chavigny recognises his error. Significantly, the correction is discursive. As Chavigny had done earlier with Mathilde, after a scene peppered with verbal sparring, Mme de Léry simply states the literal facts: 'Si vous trouvez que Mathilde a les yeux rouges, essuyez-les avec cette petite bourse que ses larmes reconnaîtront, car c'est votre bonne, brave et fidèle femme qui a passé quinze jours à la faire.'[15] Turning his own discursive strategy against him, Mme de Léry forces Chavigny to recognise the significance of the situation he himself created. The resolution, the return of Mathilde and Chavigny's pledge to tell her of his attempted seduction of her friend, underscores the importance of discourse in this play and in systems of exchange in general. Here word-play can be used to create a sort of indeterminacy (as in the failed seduction of Mme de Léry) or it can be used to diffuse indeterminacy by a cold statement of fact.

La Quenouille de Barbérine, based on the fable as told by the Italian Renaissance poet Bandello and first published in 1835, presents an even clearer example of the double use of discourse and the power imbalance of embodiedness vs. un-embodiedness. Here a young knight, Rosemberg, wagers that Ulric's wife Barbérine will be unfaithful during his absence. The *value* of a wife's fidelity is so evident that Ulric, infuriated by the

---

[15] Ibid., 448.

slander, wagers 'tout ce qu['il] possède sur terre'[16] on Barbérine's fidelity. Rosemberg promptly journeys to Ulric's château to attempt to seduce Barbérine. From the outset, Rosemberg is 'all voice'; his only proof of Barbérine's faithlessness is the commonplace 'on dit' about the faithlessness of all women. 'Je n'ai pas médit d'une femme', he explains, 'j'ai exprimé mon opinion sur toutes les femmes en général.'[17] But like Chavigny, Rosemberg will undergo an embodying transformation, as the wise Barbérine pretends to be seduced in order to administer a particularly humiliating punishment to Rosemberg: imprisoned in her tower, he is forced to spin to earn his board. 'Si vous voulez boire et manger, vous n'avez d'autre moyen que de faire comme les vieilles femmes qui gagnent leur vie en prison, c'est-à-dire de filer. Vous trouverez une quenouille et un rouet tout préparés dans cette chambre.'[18] Barbérine, speaking from offstage is now all voice and all-powerful. At her mercy is Rosemberg who falls prey to his own bodily need for food and is forced to spin. Foregrounded in this play is, of course, the issue of gender: Rosemberg's punishment is humiliating because he is not only embodied (made vulnerable) but feminised.

While discourse seems to be a sort of double-edged sword, what Scarry refers to as something that is both a tool and a weapon, in this play there is always an external, verifiable truth to which discourse refers. In *Un Caprice,* under the watchful eye of Mme de Léry, husband and wife are reunited. The essential superiority of Mathilde is recognised, as is the essential value of fidelity. Both of these plays are about coming 'to terms' in different relationships, but they both rely on artifice (play-acting) within the play to arrive successfully at their ends. As we have seen, the *mises en scène* manufactured by the characters within the plays correspond narrowly to an essentially unquestioned (though temporarily challenged) 'real', which is the value they are proving (embodying, substantiating, demonstrating) and whose proof makes its self-perpetuation possible. This will not be true of the other plays we will dis-

---

[16] Ibid., 313.
[17] Ibid., 312.
[18] Ibid., 322.

cuss in this chapter, plays which question the very system of exchange more radically and conclude much more uneasily.

Part Two. Performing Indeterminacy: Vigny's Quitte pour la peur *and Dumas'* Kean

While the plays we have discussed up to this point involved the (re)substantiation of values, we have seen that the values in flux are only placed into question by certain characters who (willingly or ignorantly) transgress the social order. The situation is set right when these characters are forced to acknowledge the truth that they had refused to see before, that is the now-substantiated claim of the value of the social order. The plays we will discuss in this section, however, have a more uneasy relationship to truth and especially to order, as *Quitte pour la peur*'s chilly reception at its initial performance will show. They explore some of the same issues of proof through some of the same techniques of *mise en scène* but the result is a much more tentative, much less 'substantial' conclusion.

Alfred de Vigny's (1797–1863) reputation as a poet was solidified with the publication of the *Poèmes antiques et modernes* in 1826. He went on to become a successful dramatist and novelist, and was an important voice in the Romantic movement. His first produced play was an adaptation of *Othello, Le More de Venise*, whose 1829 production at the Comédie Française marked an early Romantic victory on the national stage. His dramatic career lasted only six years, from 1829–1835, and his dramatic œuvre includes only six plays: three plays in verse, adapted from Shakespeare, and three plays in prose. He is known and studied today more as a poet than as a playwright, although his 1835 prose play *Chatterton* (which we will discuss at length in the third section of this chapter) represents one of the highest achievements of the Romantic period.

Quitte pour la peur, which opened at the Opéra in 1833, starred Marie Dorval, who was Vigny's mistress and major star of the boulevard theatres, and Bocage, who created many important roles in the Romantic theatre. When the play was not a great success at its premier, Vigny blamed the audience, noting in his journal: '[La multitude] a réussi à comprendre l'événement mais n'a pas compris la satire philosophique, et la question sociale lui a échappé'.[19] In fact, Vigny's play was rather an ambitious and somewhat ironic treatment of the 'proverb' genre, an eighteenth-century comic genre, perfected by Carmontelle and usually performed only in salons.[20] Gérard Dessons defines the genre thus: '[Le proverbe] consiste en l'illustration dramatique d'une vérité morale, posée dès le départ, qui règle le déroulement de la pièce et signifie la fin'.[21] But Vigny's proverb, as we will see, is not so straightforward; rather, it upsets the audience's expectations to present a subversive moral clothed in a form that is usually diverting but, as we saw with *Un Caprice* and *La Quenouille de Barbérine*, far from challenging.

Still, the plot of the play is simple: La Duchesse has not seen her husband since their wedding three years ago. His long-standing relationship to La Marquise, who never appears, takes precedence over a marriage contracted for economic reasons. Following the example of those around her, La Duchesse has also taken a lover, and as the play opens, we find her terrified that she may be pregnant. Her suspicions are confirmed after a visit with her doctor, who then informs Le Duc of his wife's condition. Rather than exact revenge or enact punishment, he pays a visit to his wife, spending the night in her bedroom talking with her to save appearances. He leaves in the morning, still not knowing his wife's first name, but having saved her reputation.

The play is set during the reign of Louis XVI, a decadent court where hypocrisy is the rule of the day and appearances are more important than reality. As the play opens, La Duchesse finds herself at loose ends, waiting for word from the doctor or from her lover, Le Chevalier. As she waits for verification of her suspicions, she ponders what would happen to her if her pregnancy were to become evident:

[19] Alfred de Vigny, *Œuvres complètes II* (Paris: Gallimard, 1948), 989.
[20] In the notes to the Vigny, *Œuvres complètes I* (Paris: Gallimard, 1986), editors François Germain and André Jarry suggest that Vigny's proverb was eventually successful in its 1849 revival at the Gymnase because '... le goût des spectateurs avait donc changé. Depuis l'année précédente, en effet, on jouait les proverbes de Musset' (Vigny, I, 1473).
[21] Gérard Dessons, 'La parole du siècle dans les Proverbes de Musset', *Travaux de Littérature*, 4 (1991), 197–207.

Est-ce un état bien heureux que celui où l'on sent que si l'on était mère on en mourrait de honte ... que tous ceux qui me passent l'oubli d'un mari ne me passeraient pas l'oubli de son nom, car ce n'est qu'un nom qu'il faut respecter, et ce nom vous tient enchaînée, ce nom est suspendu sur votre tête comme une épée.[22]

La Duchesse enunciates here the most important theme of the play: the theme of the name. Just as in the plays of Musset we discussed above, power lies on the side of the word, the name, the voice. To be embodied is to be restricted as La Duchesse is in the opening scene where her maid reminds her that the doctor has forbidden her to write, to ride or to sing. Moreover, her body will, as the pregnancy develops, come to stand as proof of adultery, which proof must banish her from society. It is the age-old story: the woman is trapped by the proof of adultery marked on her body in the pregnancy, while the man is engaged only in name and then only if he so chooses.

The situation is exaggerated here, where La Duchesse's only link to her husband is his name. She asks her maid,

M'expliquerais-tu bien ce que c'est précisément qu'un maître inconnu qu'il me faut respecter, craindre et aimer comme Dieu, sans le voir ... qui ne se soucie de moi nullement ... qui me donne seulement son nom à porter de bien loin, comme une terre abandonnée?[23]

While Vigny has chosen an Ancien Régime setting — presumably because the Ancien Régime worked as short-hand for hypocrisy and decadence — he shows himself here to be sympathetic to the plight of women in his contemporary society, where proof of an adulterous liaison would still cause a woman to be banished from the ranks of high society. As the doctor puts it: 'Madame, quand une jeune femme a une faiblesse publique, tout le monde a son pardon dans le cœur et sa condamnation sur les lèvres. ... Ce n'est pas la faute qui est punie c'est le bruit qu'elle fait.'[24]

[22] Vigny, I, 726.
[23] Ibid., 725.
[24] Ibid., 729.

For Le Duc, whose idea of honour consists of 'le soin de soutenir la dignité de son nom',[25] we might expect, as La Duchesse fears, that he will choose to engage his body and kill his wife's lover in a duel or even kill his wife to protect his name. La Duchesse hints at a deeper fear as well, the fear of rape. When Le Duc arrives at her door and seems to be in rather gay spirits, she implores her maid to kill her: 'Il ne peut venir que par fureur ou par passion; de toute façon, c'est me faire mourir. Tue-moi, je t'en prie.'[26] But if the fault of La Duchesse lies only in the disgrace of the name, Le Duc finds a way to repair the fault in name only, through a performance of conjugal intimacy.

When he arrives, as we have seen, La Duchesse is not at all aware of her husband's plan. In fact he rather toys with her throughout their scene together, which takes up about the last third of the play. He plays several roles with her, trying to find the one that suits their relationship best. At first, he acts as if their meeting is not out of the ordinary. When this meets with reticence from his frightened wife, he hints at the sort of frankness he will show at the end of the scene: 'Ce n'est pas cette docilité qu'il me faut, c'est de la franchise.'[27] In fact, Le Duc is not himself ready for frankness; lighting on her copy of Voltaire's *Zaïre*, he introduces some overt play-acting, as he suggests they read together. 'Tenez (nous avons le temps), si vous étiez la belle Zaïre, soupçonnée d'infidélité par Orosmane, le violent, le terrible Orosmane.'[28] When he reads a speech of Orosmane's full of jealous rage and unrequited love, La Duchesse is sure he means to kill her and calls off the play-acting with: 'Monsieur! avez-vous quelque chose à me reprocher?..'. Not through teasing his wife, Le Duc replies '... que dites-vous donc là? Ce n'est pas dans la pièce.'[29] Just as in the first scene, before learning for certain that she is pregnant, La Duchesse here is suffering from indeterminacy. She does not know for

[25] Ibid., 744.
[26] Ibid., 737. We can hardly take seriously the demand that Rosette, the most frankly comic character of the play, kill her mistress. Still, as Germain and Jarry remark in their notes to the Pléiade edition, the very serious fear of rape runs throughout La Duchesse's speeches, see Vigny, I, 730 and 1476, n.1.
[27] Vigny, I, 739.
[28] Ibid., 740.
[29] Ibid.

certain whether Le Duc knows of her pregnancy, and she does not know what his intentions are. La Duchesse tries to force the moment to its crisis by asking him outright, but Le Duc continues to deflect literality: partly, as we saw in the episode with *Zaïre*, just to pass the time until morning, by playing the role of husband.

When he begins to talk about his ancestors (whose portraits decorate the room), and about the family name he hopes to pass on, he stumbles across a subject about which his wife has much to say. '...c'est de votre nom qu'il s'agit, et non du mien',[30] she reminds him. Again, the theme of the name is central to the question of power in the relationship. While his own family name is the abstract value for which he would sacrifice anything, and which he is there to protect, Le Duc reveals his own weakness here when we find that he does not know his own wife's first name. Emboldened by his error, La Duchesse reproaches Le Duc for not caring for her and refuses to tell him her real name, explaining that first-names are meant to be known and used only by people who love each other. While it is the premise of the play that the couple are not in love and were married for the sake of their families, La Duchesse's remark still stings. For if it is acceptable that they have both transgressed their wedding vows physically in adultery, Le Duc's error shows that failing in the name, in the appearance, of marriage is unacceptable. They are not put on equal footing by Le Duc's much lighter fault, but the momentary advantage gained by La Duchesse allows her to open up a discussion of the real terms of their marriage and of marriage in their society. This is where the play eschews the expected dénouement of a traditional proverb and instead of realigning an idea with an object (fidelity, the happy couple), revels in revealing the irreparable breach.

La Duchesse highlights the cleft between concrete and abstract when she asks the central question of the play: 'Qu'est-ce que ce mariage du nom et de la fortune, d'où les personnes sont absentes, et pourquoi nos hommes d'affaires nous ont fait paraître dans ce marché?' Le Duc can only answer her by describing their decadent society in which 'la religion (irréparable malheur peut-être!) s'en est allée en plaisanterie, fondue avec

---

[30] Ibid., 742.

le sel attique dans le creuset des philosophes.'³¹ They seem to agree that marriage, love, religion, and all the abstract ideals of their society, used to be based on something real, but have become corrupt and meaningless. How, then, can they make them real again? I have argued that performance serves as a way to lend such abstractions a temporary reality, by illustrating the idea through a physical presence. But Le Duc's response to the corruption of his society is rather a blind faith in yet another abstraction: 'Dirigeons-nous seulement, lorsqu'il faudra, selon cette loi que, ma foi, je ne vis jamais nulle par écrite mais que je sentis toujours vivante en moi, la loi de l'Honneur.'³²

His performance in coming to his wife's house obeys the law of honour by protecting the family name, but only in appearance. The child born to La Duchesse can now be his heir, but will not biologically be his son, and this is enough. Le Duc's performance does not attempt anything so ambitious as to repair his marriage, only the less ambitious task of making it appear so for the world. Le Duc goes so far as to kneel down and ask La Duchesse to forgive him for neglecting her, but then '*brusquement, en homme, et comme quittant le masque*',³³ he reveals that they have both been playing a scene for an unseen audience (their servants and by extension their peers). He then asks her to shake on it, to conclude the deal, explaining: 'Dans une société qui se corrompt et se dissout chaque jour comme la nôtre, tout ce qui reste encore de possible, c'est le respect des convenances. Il y a des occasions où la dissimulation est presque sainte.'³⁴ He thus reaffirms their marriage as a business arrangement between two people with common interests (and a common name). The message is rather subversive; for while we expect to see the reunion of a happy couple, substantiating the value of conjugal fidelity for us all, the play gives us a happy couple, united only by friendship born of a night of dissimulation and fully intending to persist in their adultery. Whereas the characters in the other plays we have discussed used playacting to set

[31] Ibid., 743.
[32] Ibid., 744.
[33] Ibid., 745.
[34] Ibid.

things right, here they use playacting to set things to looking right and are satisfied with the power and freedom this gives them.

Like Le Duc and La Duchesse in *Quitte pour la peur*, the title character in Dumas' *Kean ou Désordre et génie*, an English Shakespearean actor, makes an uneasy peace with appearances, as the play-acting within this five-act comedy occasions an almost infinite *mise en abyme* of the actor's practice. Alexandre Dumas, *père*, born in 1802, was himself a man of the theatre and in financial terms the most successful playwright of the Romantic era. Produced in 1836 at the Variétés, *Kean* was Dumas' last major hit, but followed successes in the melodrama as early as 1825 and in *drames* such as *Henri III et sa cour* in 1829, *Antony* and *Richard Darlington* in 1831, and *La Tour de Nesle* in 1832. Still, Dumas' plays are rather dated and are very seldom read and even more seldom performed today. *Kean* is a notable exception, as it was revived in an adaptation by Jean-Paul Sartre in 1953. It is Dumas' novels, including *Le Comte de Monte Cristo* and *Les Trois Mousquetaires*, which won him immense popularity during his lifetime and which have assured him worldwide recognition since his death in 1870.

F.W.J. Hemmings reports in his 1979 biography of Dumas that the playwright saw the subject of *Kean*, Edmund Kean (1787–1833), in *Hamlet*, *Romeo and Juliet*, and *Othello* in 1827, when a group of English actors came to Paris to perform Shakespeare.[35] This was an important moment both for Dumas and for Romantic theatre in general, as the Shakespearean forms provided a needed infusion of novelty into the French theatrical scene. The success of the Shakespearean plays in Paris later spurred the authors of the *drame* to demand greater official recognition and certainly contributed to the Bataille d'*Hernani* in 1830. By 1836, when *Kean* was first performed, the Romantic ascendancy on the stage (in both dramatic form and stagecraft) was assured, but Dumas uses a play about an actor to explore the questions of stagecraft, of mask and performance in a way that destabilises the ground that the Romantics had conquered. Largely refraining from employing the easy machinery of the

---

[35] F.W.J. Hemmings, *Alexandre Dumas: The King of Romance* (New York: Charles Scribner's Sons, 1979), 51.

melodrama, which plays a part in most of his work, Dumas turns the stage around to reveal the inner workings of the theatre. The result is, in the opinion of many critics, his greatest theatrical achievement.

While Dumas himself categorised *Kean* as a comedy, Anne Ubersfeld refers to it repeatedly as a *drame* and Dorothy McCall calls it a melodrama.[36] They are all right: *Kean* is a hybrid genre, fusing elements of *drame* and melodrama with a distinctly comedic happy ending. The rather complex plot is basically about unrequited love: Lord Mewill's love for Anna, Anna's love for Kean, Kean's love for Elena. The work of the play will be to settle each character with the correct partner and to punish the evil-doers along the way. All of this takes place under the watchful eye of Kean's close friend, the Prince of Wales, who in the end plays the part of the *deus ex machina* to resolve the complications of the plot. Still, as in *Quitte pour la peur*, performance will not necessarily substantiate or concretise abstract values but will allow the characters to use illusion to their own ends.

Throughout the play, Kean is shown in many different situations: as lover of Elena (countess and wife of the Danish ambassador), as friend of the Prince of Wales, as patron of a poor family of acrobats, as mentor of Anna (a rich orphan who wants to become an actress). But in all of these parts he is playing a role; above all, Kean is the actor who has, whatever else, to perform. With Elena he is Romeo and later, overtaken by jealousy, Othello; to the prince he is Falstaff; to the poor he is Prince Hal, and to Anna, he is Hamlet, prince of the stage. Though loved and respected by Elena and the Prince of Wales, Kean's status as a professional performer relegates him to a marginal position in their society. He is accepted among them first as a jester, and only conditionally as lover and friend. Ironically the fame and talent, which granted him access to the upper-class salons, will always keep him from truly belonging there. At the same time, originally a man of the people, the wealthy and successful Kean no longer belongs among the people. So as not to cause a stir in the Act III baptism at which he is to be the godfather, Kean is forced to dis-

---

[36] See Anne Ubersfeld, *Le Drame romantique* (Paris: Berlin, 1993), 131–2 and Dorothy McCall, *The Theatre of Jean-Paul Sartre* (New York: Columbia University, 1967), 98–109.

guise himself in more humble clothing than he is now used to wearing. This is a common portrait of the romantic hero: a man, set apart by genius, struggling to find a place in society without betraying his gift.[37] To leave the stage is impossible: 'Moi! moi! quitter le théâtre... moi! Oh! vous ne savez donc pas ce que c'est que cette robe de Nessus qu'on ne peut arracher de dessus ses épaules qu'en déchirant sa propre chair?'[38] But to remain is to choose marginalisation.

What Anna tries to show Kean is that his genius gives him a Christ-like transformative power to transcend the restrictive reality of salon society. Just as he transforms himself into Romeo, Othello or Hamlet on stage, his art transforms the present for those who watch him. She explains that, dying (literally) of *ennui*, she was taken to theatre, where: 'Je me tournai instinctivement, [vers la scène] cherchant de l'air à respirer... C'est alors que j'entendis une voix ... oh! ...qui vibra jusqu'au fond de mon cœur.'[39] It was, of course, Kean 'qui avait ressuscité la jeune fille déjà couchée dans la tombe.'[40] Anna's recovery stands as physical proof of the extraordinary power of Kean's acting and of the sacred nature of the theatre for those sensitive enough to commune there.

If Kean is Christ on stage, off stage he is a bit player in the society to which he aspires. From the stage, he is able to heal the dying Anna, but off stage, when called upon to defend her honour from Lord Mewill, he is not altogether effective. He does foil the abduction plan by which Mewill hoped to make Anna marry him against her will, but Mewill refuses to fight him in a duel, as the actor is too far beneath him. Similarly, when he woos Elena on stage in the role of Romeo or Othello, she is transformed and feels love for him, but his off-stage courtship is a failure. The only time Kean's actions have an effect in the world is when he is performing on stage. Rather than the site of mere make-believe and illusion, the stage is the only space in which Kean experiences real (if transcribed and temporary) power.

---

[37] This is the portrait of Vigny's *Chatterton*, of Musset's *Fantasio* and of Balzac's Balthazar in *La Recherche de l'absolu* among many others in every genre.
[38] Alexandre Dumas, *Théâtre complet* (Paris: Colman Lévy, 1889), V, 134.
[39] Ibid., 153.
[40] Ibid., 154

In Kean's final performance (the Act IV play within a play), the boundary between stage and hall is utterly abolished and the audience is engaged to perform in the play. After scene viii, '*Le toile tombe; au moment où elle a touché le plancher, le Régisseur passe par devant, et vient jusqu'au milieu de l'avant-scène.*'⁴¹ He apologises for the delay to the audience of Drury Lane (played by the audience of Dumas' *Kean*) and announces the play they are about to see; then, the curtain goes back up on the nightingale / lark scene from *Romeo and Juliet*. When Kean has his breakdown (on seeing the Prince of Wales enter Elena's box) and comes out of character, *Romeo and Juliet* recedes, as Kean acknowledges a reality outside of the stage. But that reality is still part of the play *Kean* and so still belongs to the fictional realm. Dumas' audacious dramaturgy, in making the audience physically play a part in *Kean*, levels out the realities we usually negotiate as audience.⁴² Rather than standing in for our world, the world of *Kean* becomes our world as we stand (or sit) in it. Only the curtain, which falls at the same time on Kean's disastrous performance and *Kean's* Act IV re-establishes the limits between the fictional world and our world.

The effect of this scene is dual. First, on the level of the plot of *Kean*, this scene leads to the actor's exile and ironically prepares the happy ending, in which he leaves for New York with Anna. Second, it engages the audience in an examination of the actor's practice, as the stage temporarily expands to include the hall and by extension the audience and their world. If performance is no longer a diversion *from* the world and its cares, if it comes to have an effect *in* the world (as Kean's performance has had in his world all along), then the theatre is a privileged site, where illusion can affect reality. Dumas is, in fact, challenging his audience to transform their own reality, to imagine a better world, where the artist is

---

⁴¹ Ibid., 182.
⁴² For a present-day audience, this dramaturgy would not be so very audacious, but in Dumas' theatre, the audience is rarely even acknowledged, and a game that implicates the audience is entirely novel. Even Sartre, in his 1953 adaptation of the play, figures the audience of Drury Lane on the stage, rather than requiring his audience to play the part.

accepted fully in society and society allows itself to be transformed by art's power.

Kean does not live in such a world. He finds that even in the theatre, where he felt himself omnipotent, it is the Prince who holds the real power. It is the Prince who finally ends Kean's raillery, by calling for the curtain. Kean's power is limited by the stage, the space in which he embodies princes and lovers. The Prince, on the other hand, holds unlimited power, because everything he does is 'behind the scenes'. The Prince's invisible hand guides the resolution to the cascading dilemmas presented in Act V. First, Anna visits Kean but must hide when Elena arrives. After a tender scene, Elena breaks off their affair, but must also hide when her husband arrives. He is there to challenge Kean because he believes he has proof of their affair. A letter from the Prince arrives mysteriously just in time to satisfy the ambassador that he was mistaken and he leaves. Then Kean plans an old comedic trick to get Elena safely home: he will send her out dressed as Anna, but when he goes to fetch her, he finds her mysteriously gone. The Prince finally arrives in person to explain: he was aware of everything going on in the actor's home, sent the letter to save Elena, and had her taken out by a back way. He has also arranged for Kean to be exiled rather than imprisoned. The official story here is whatever the prince makes it, and everybody is a player in his world, wittingly or otherwise.

Kean's exile represents not so much banishment from his society, for he had never really belonged, but the possibility of escape to republican America, where he might be free from his society's constraints. In the Old World, meaning hangs from the delicate thread of the Prince's will; *Kean* holds out the hope that in the New World, the artist will be the maker of meaning. The play's optimism rests on shaky ground, however, since it is still only through performance, through illusion, that the artist can hope to transform his reality. Dumas' play shows all the power and vulnerability of performance and finally substantiates for us the power and vulnerability of the artist.

Unlike Musset's plays in which performance unproblematically evacuates the problem of indeterminacy,[43] *Quitte pour la peur* and *Kean* present performance as a way to keep doubt and the possibility of individual freedom alive. Through his performance, Le Duc in Vigny's play introduces a doubt as to the paternity of his wife's child, allowing them both to continue their extramarital affairs with impunity. Through his many performances, Kean introduces a doubt as to the justice of the social structure and creates an opening for the individual to act in his world. In both plays, the characters find a way of negotiating, through the falseness of performance, the falseness and arbitrariness of the world. This element of social critique presents a challenge to the *status quo* and forces the audience to recognise the gap that persists between what is real and what is imagined.

Part Three. *Performing Resistance: Dumas'* Antony *and Vigny's* Chatterton

Up to this point, we have discussed plays in which performance within the play serves either the function of analogical verification for some abstract value or the function of keeping analogical verification at bay, of keeping meaning afloat and value in question, the better to negotiate a corrupt system. In this last section of the chapter we will discuss two plays in which the values of the world, established from the outset, are so oppressive that the heroes prefer neither to reaffirm nor to manipulate them, but to resist them entirely. Their refusal to perform which, itself, becomes a kind of performance, will substantiate not society's values, but the values held by the individuals. As we will see, the individual is crushed under the weight of the world's demands and is reintegrated, despite himself, into the system of meaning he rejected in life.

---

[43]   I am referring here only to the plays of Musset discussed in this chapter. In fairness to Musset, it should be noted that many of his plays (including some in the proverb genre) and including *La Nuit Vénitienne, Il ne faut jurer de rien, Le Chandelier,* and *A quoi rêvent les jeunes filles,* problematise performance in ways altogether as interesting as is found in the works of Vigny and Dumas.

First performed at the Théâtre de la Porte-Saint-Martin in 1831 and starring Marie Dorval and Bocage (who would later create the roles of La Duchesse and Le Duc in *Quitte pour la peur*) *Antony* was perhaps the greatest financial success of the 1830s. Combining aspects of melodrama with a more deeply traumatised, distinctly romantic hero, it exemplifies the *drame contemporain*, of which it was the first major production. Antony is a young man of obscure parentage who returns to Paris society after an absence of three years to see Adèle, the woman he loved, now married to another. From the moment of their first meeting at the end of Act I, the two are obviously still in love, but Adèle, wishing to remain faithful to her husband, a military officer in another town, flees Antony at every opportunity. At the end of Act III, he stops her in her flight toward her husband and rapes her in an inn. Three months later, Act IV shows them as a happy couple, but at the mercy of gossips who would ruin Adèle's reputation. The play reaches its climax in Act V, when Adèle's husband returns just as she and Antony are preparing to run away together. Adèle prefers to die rather than live dishonoured and so Antony kills her and proclaims, as her husband enters: 'Elle me résistait, je l'ai assassinée!'[44]

Like Kean, Antony associates with members of high society, without ever truly belonging. Although his parents supply him with money through a lawyer, he does not know their, and by extension his own, identity. Three years before the action of the play, during his original romance with Adèle, he had deceived himself into believing his birth did not matter; but since her marriage to the Colonel d'Hervey, he recognises that his own outcast status is irreparable. Speaking of the impossibility of marriage (and therefore the impossibility of integration into the social order)

---

[44] Alexandre Dumas, *Antony* (Paris: Éditions de la Table Ronde, 1994), 151. This line (in alexandrine verse) caused such a sensation that Dumas reports in his memoirs that, on one occasion, the audience railed because the line was accidentally cut when the stage manager mistakenly brought down the curtain too early. Despite the boos of the audience, Bocage refused to go back on stage to pronounce the famous words, so Marie Dorval sat up and said, 'Vous le voyez, Messieurs, je lui résistais, il m'a assassinée' and then died again. Apparently, the audience was satisfied. Alexandre Dumas, *Mes Mémoires* (Paris: Gallimard, 1967), 4, cxcix, 302.

for orphans and those without a family name, Antony bitterly states society's point of view: 'Il faut que le malheureux reste malheureux; pour lui, Dieu n'a pas de regard, les hommes de pitié.'[45] Though powerless to change the *status quo* to which Antony refers, Adèle is certainly not without pity for her former lover. She sees his marginal position not as a mark of inferior birth but of spiritual superiority. She explains to her sister Clara her initial attraction to him thus:

> Si tu l'avais suivi comme moi au milieu du monde, où il semblait étranger, parce qu'il lui était supérieur; si tu l'avais vu triste et sévère au milieu de ces jeunes fous, élégants et nuls; ... si, au milieu de ces regards qui, le soir, nous entourent, joyeux et pétillants, ... tu avais vu ses yeux constamment arrêtés sur toi, fixes et sombres, tu aurais deviné que l'amour qu'ils exprimaient ne se laissait pas abattre par quelques difficultés.[46]

This is a common trait of the romantic hero: the young man is in conflict with his society because of inferiority they observe, but also at a deeper level the hero possesses a superiority they refuse to recognise. For Adèle, Antony's superiority consists of a gravity of manner and a steadiness of feeling, which make it impossible for him to hide his true emotions.[47] The theme of false love (perfectly acceptable in society because easy to dissimulate) and criminal, true love (which cannot but express itself in ways inappropriate to society) plays a central role in our examination of performance in this play; for while Antony and Adèle refuse on one level to perform (to pretend not to be in love), on another, deeper level, their love cannot help but perform itself.

Throughout the play, Antony makes his love real to Adèle and to the audience by engaging his body in the process of analogical verification. He first sees Adèle again when he saves her life, throwing himself in front of her horses, which have gone wild. An injured Antony is carried into Adèle's house to recover and there in Act I, scene vi, they share their

---

[45] Dumas, *Antony* (1994), 59.
[46] Ibid., 19.
[47] Dumas's biographer, Claude Schopp and other critics, also see Antony as a semi-autographical portrait of Dumas. Claude Shopp, *Alexandre Dumas* (Paris: Fayard, 2002).

first *tête-à-tête* of the play. They speak explicitly about the falseness of the world, about the performance of happiness required by society, which recognises only physical injury as real and finds in spiritual injury a subject of jest. 'Et c'est pour cela', he concludes, 'que Dieu a voulu que l'homme ne pût cacher le sang de son corps sous ses vêtements, mais a permis qu'il cachât les blessures de son âme sous un sourire.'[48] When he learns that she plans to have him moved, since he is not in any real danger and his staying might arouse suspicions about adultery, Antony rips off the bandages covering his injuries, reopening his wounds and then, as Act I ends, faints from the blood loss. In this way, Antony creates a physical wound to substantiate the spiritual wound he feels in the loss of Adèle and at the same time creates a cover story for his continued presence in her house.

Later, in Act III, Adèle's body will be the site of substantiation of Antony's power, as Antony perpetrates a rape that binds Adèle to him. The rape takes place in an inn as Adèle, having confessed her regard for Antony in Act II and promised to meet him the next day, flees him for the protection of her husband. She is not afraid of Antony as much as she is afraid of her own feelings for him and her own weakness. Antony, alerted to her flight, arrives at the inn first and arranges for there to be no way for Adèle to leave. He hires and sends away all the horses and rents every room in the hotel, so as to force her into a room that shares a balcony with his. Later, he breaks a pane of glass on the balcony door on Adèle's side and enters her room, dragging her into an inner room as she cries for help. This use of space is reminiscent of melodrama, where every door, trap door and balcony on stage serves a purpose in advancing the plot, in what Ubersfeld calls 'un espace machiné et machiné pour l'action'.[49] The result here, however, is entirely romantic, as the codes governing melodrama would protect the heroine from rape.

The consummation of their affair in rape is important for several reasons. Adèle as victim stands as the physical sign of Antony's violent desire. Earlier, Antony spoke about Adèle's new last name: 'je désap–

---

[48] Dumas, *Antony* (1994), 38.
[49] Anne Ubersfeld, 'Alexandre Dumas, père, et le drame bourgeois', *Cahiers de l'Association internationale des études françaises*, 35 (mai 1983), 123.

prendrai le nom d'Adèle pour celui de d'Hervey... Madame d'Hervey! et que le malheur d'une vie tout entière soit dans ces deux mots!'⁵⁰ Here, he marks Adèle as his in a way that is more real (more substantial) than the mere name of d'Hervey. Later, when rape turns to murder, Adèle's dead body will once again become the site of substantiation of Antony's criminal passion. More disturbing, perhaps, than the rape, itself, is Adèle's subsequent behaviour in continuing the liaison with her rapist and later in asking him to kill her. As distasteful as this outdated, romanticised view of rape may be, I think we must read the rape here not only as the performance of Antony's dominance, but also as the substantiation of the violence of Adèle's desire for Antony. In the introduction to his edition of the play, Pierre-Louis Rey goes so far as to dismiss the rape as a theatrical convention which fooled no one: 'C'est ... au nom de conventions un peu trop transparentes que serait qualifiée de 'viol' la consommation de l'adultère'.⁵¹ If we believe the message of the play, that a woman's adultery, if discovered, would bring universal condemnation, then the fact that the affair begins with rape allows the audience of 1831 a moral loophole; they may excuse Adèle's subsequent adultery with Antony, since, after all, she could not help herself.

That she is powerless over Antony and over her love is eventually Adèle's downfall, as she is unable to dissimulate her passion. La Vicomtesse de Lacy, Adèle's friend, serves as a model of what a woman's behaviour *should* be, if she hopes to escape detection in adultery. The difference lies, as her latest lover Eugène d'Hervilly explains, in the nature of her love. While Adèle and Antony share a true love, La Vicomtesse and Eugène simply play at love: 'Vous commandez une robe, vous me dites que vous m'aimez, vous allez au bal...votre cœur reste libre, votre tête est folle.'⁵² For La Vicomtesse and her lovers, the performance of love is an amusement, a diversion from the exigencies of daily life; for Antony and Adèle, love is the only real on which the exigencies of the world never cease to intrude.

[50] Dumas, *Antony* (1994), 35.
[51] Alexandre Dumas, *Antony*, Pierre-Louis Rey (ed.) (Paris: Gallimard, 2002), 22.
[52] Dumas, *Antony* (1994), 107.

During the scene at the ball, Antony and Adèle find themselves a spectacle for the entertainment of the other guests, as their story has been fodder for the gossips since Adèle's precipitous return from the inn. At Antony's entrance the stage direction reads: '*Tout le monde se retourne. Les yeux se fixent alternativement sur Adèle et sur Antony qui entre...*'.[53] Just then, the conversation turns significantly to the theatre and to the work of Eugène, who is a poet of the Romantic school. The ladies exhort him to take up a contemporary subject, but Eugène explains that the audience would find fault with any contemporary play, as 'la ressemblance entre le héros et le parterre sera trop grande, l'analogie trop intime'.[54] The analogy indeed grows intimate as the catty Mme de Camps suggests a ready-made contemporary plot for the theatre, the plot of *Antony*. Her not so subtle references to Adèle's behaviour excite Antony's ire, but in polite company he can only defend Adèle by offering further details, suggesting that if she has compromised herself it is not through lack of honesty, but lack of guile.

Their only defence against the world 'qui nous entoure de tous ses liens, qui nous épie de tous ces yeux'[55] and which puts them thus on display is to withdraw entirely from it and that is what Antony suggests in Act V, when they learn that Adèle's husband is on his way back to Paris. They briefly caress a dream of escape from the prying eyes of the world but find that escape is impossible: if Adèle could endure the life of a fallen woman, withdrawn from society, she cannot impose that stigma on her daughter, who would suffer in her stead the same fate Antony has suffered. They consider the ultimate withdrawal in a double suicide, which Adèle at first finds tempting: 'Oh! oui, cette mort avec toi, l'éternité dans tes bras... Oh! ce serait le ciel';[56] but they reject that plan, as they realise that their bodies found together would serve as proof of their adultery and leave a posthumous stain on Adèle's honour. Finally, they arrive at the plan they carry out: Antony will kill Adèle and then

[53] Ibid., 116.
[54] Ibid., 120.
[55] Ibid., 130.
[56] Ibid., 147.

claim she resisted him. That he remains alive to be tried and guillotined will be proof enough of the veracity of his claim.

This is the only dissimulation to which the two ever submit and it requires the total surrender of both of their bodies to make it believable. To her husband and to the world, Adèle's death will prove that she was the virtuous woman they always knew she was and Antony's crime will prove him to be the heartless rogue everyone suspected him of being all along. In this sense, their performance is surrender to the beliefs of the world which the two had obviously rejected in life. But in another sense, their final performance is transcendent because, different from the world at large or from Adèle's husband who see only the body, we the audience are there in the closed bedroom as witness to the truth of Antony's heroic character and the realness of Adèle's boundless love. We understand what the world cannot: that Adèle's death is a sacrifice, sanctifying their love and expiating its sin. As in *Kean*, the audience stands in opposition to the world at large, forming a 'happy few' of Romantics who understand and recognise a deeper real.

Like Antony, Chatterton, the eponymous hero of Vigny's 1835 *drame contemporain*, finds himself at the mercy of an uncomprehending society. He, too, resists performing according to the norms demanded by the superficial majority, and instead dreams of withdrawing entirely to the pure realm of poetry. Vigny's play stages the last day in the life of the English poet Thomas Chatterton (1752–1770) who, reduced to poverty, committed suicide. In Vigny's version, presented at the Comédie Française to tremendous popular appreciation but rather tepid reviews, Vigny respects the unities of time, place and action, distilling the story to that of 'un homme qui écrit une lettre le matin, et qui attend la réponse jusqu'au soir; elle arrive, et le tue'.[57] In Chatterton, as he explains in the play's preface, 'La Dernière nuit de travail', Vigny saw not so much a historical figure, but the universal figure of the poet, sacrificed to the material exigencies of the world. Poetry is the language by which that world might be transcended and transformed, if only people were open to its transformative powers. Vigny writes of his own earlier work *Stello*, also the story of a

---

[57] Vigny, I, 759.

poet: 'Beaucoup ont lu ce livre et l'ont aimé comme livre, mais peu de cœurs, hélas! en ont été changés.'[58] Chatterton's personal tragedy was his failure to transform his readers through poetry; *Chatterton*'s utopian promise is its potential to transcend the individuality of the members of the audience, to unite them in terror and pity, to form them into an alternate community who recognise the worth of the poet.

Chatterton, like Antony, refuses to play the role that society has assigned him because on the one hand, he rejects the superficiality and forced gaiety of the world, and on the other, he finds it impossible not to show his true, pensive character. In his first appearance he explains: 'Pour moi, j'ai résolu de ne me point masquer et d'être moi-même jusqu'à la fin, d'écouter, en tout, mon cœur...et de me résigner à bien accomplir ma loi.'[59] Chatterton differs from Antony in his experience of marginalisation, for while Antony resents his liminal status, Chatterton seeks it out. He is living as a boarder in a bourgeois home, fairly hidden from everyone who knows him. Moreover, when he arrived at the home of his hosts, John and Kitty Bell, he gave them only one name, Mr. Thomas. In this way, until Lord Talbot arrives and recognises him in Act II, he avoids any association with his family name, any expectation of what his character or behaviour will be. He is entirely free to behave according to 'his law'.

Much of Chatterton's diffidence in society relates to his view of poetry, his desire (which mirrors that of Vigny's) that his poetry be the instrument of change in the hearts of his readers, rather than mere entertainment. In his long soliloquy in Act III, he describes two possible types of poetry, one pure and the other corrupt:

> Il faut ... que ma volonté soit assez puissante pour saisir mon âme et l'emporter tour à tour dans le cadavre ressuscité des personnages que j'évoque ... ou bien, il faut que devant Chatterton malade, devant Chatterton qui a froid, qui a faim, ma volonté fasse poser avec prétention un autre Chatterton, gracieusement paré pour l'amusement public ... Voilà les deux poésies possibles

---

[58] Ibid., 749.
[59] Ibid., 771.

... les divertir ou leur faire pitié; faire jouer de misérables poupées, ou l'être soi-même et faire trafic de cette singerie!⁶⁰

Though Chatterton expresses contempt for a poetry corrupted by uncomprehending readers and the commercialisation of the enterprise, at this point in the play he is reduced to betraying his own beliefs. In order to pay his debts, Chatterton must write. 'Il ne s'agit plus de sourire et d'être bon! de saluer et de serrer la main! Toute cette comédie est jouée: j'en commence une autre avec moi-même.'⁶¹ The other comedy is to play the role of the man who writes for money, but it is a role that Chatterton is unable to play. By the end of the scene, he has formed another plan to pay his debts: if the Lord Maire (to whom he wrote that morning) does not offer to help him, he will commit suicide and have his body sold for scientific experiments. This drastic solution, which he explains in apostrophe to his dead father, allows Chatterton to reclaim his family name and to keep it pure; it will not be associated with a man in debtor's prison, nor with a hack writer of light verse.

Chatterton's belief in the purity of poetic language mirrors a mistrust of ordinary language, which is one of the major themes of the play. Although when the play opens, he is already in love with Kitty Bell and she with him, they have never spoken to one another. She scolds her daughter for having accepted a Bible as a gift from him, saying: '... depuis trois mois qu'il loge ici, je ne lui ai même pas parlé une fois, et vous avez accepté quelque chose, un livre.'⁶² In fact, if the relationship we see staged in the first two and a half acts of this three-act play is any indication, Kitty communicates with Chatterton through her children, through the exchange of objects and through the Quaker, the family friend and confidant who is present throughout most of the action. Kitty and Chatterton's first conversation together is occasioned by the careless speech of the young lords, who in Act II, scene iii, insinuate that there is an illicit relationship between Chatterton and Kitty. Both are mortified by the lords' idle talk, and Chatterton must finally break his silence with Kitty to reas-

---

[60] Ibid., 792.
[61] Ibid.
[62] Ibid., 764.

sure her that his intentions are honourable. Still, when they speak it is mostly through the Quaker, or at least in the third person. For example, Kitty says to the Quaker, 'Voici un livre que j'ai trouvé dans les mains de ma fille. Demandez à monsieur s'il ne lui appartient pas.'[63] The mediation here is double: in speaking to the Quaker she avoids addressing Chatterton directly and in implying that the Bible should be returned to him, she is hinting her displeasure with his friends in the previous scene.

The young lords represent one foil to Chatterton's demeanour; frivolous and gay, they say whatever comes to mind, just for sport. The other, more consistent contrast is between Chatterton and John Bell, Kitty's husband. From the very beginning of the play, John Bell is characterised by his voice; 'cette voix me brise le cœur',[64] Kitty tells us. In fact, we hear John Bell before we see him, as he shouts at his workers off stage before coming on stage to give them a lesson in capitalism. Again, and here on two levels, the body and voice dichotomy plays a role in the characterisation of the hero. Chatterton, characterised by his silence, even to the point of not revealing his last name, is all body. Impoverished, he is hungry; fatigued, he must still labour. John Bell the capitalist, on the other hand, is all voice. His labour is not physical, but the labour of capital; rich, he does not feel the pressing bodily needs suffered by the poor: neither cold nor hungry, John Bell is insulated by capital from his own body and its needs.

The critique of capitalism, which runs throughout the play, underscores the sterility of the capitalist system and hints at a higher law to which society as a whole should aspire.[65] John Bell defends his decision to fire an injured worker, claiming 'Je suis juste selon la loi', but the Quaker replies, 'Et ta loi, est-elle juste selon Dieu?'[66] Likewise, the utility principle around which John Bell has organised his household is anathema to the poet, who sees a higher good than utility in human endeavour. The Qua-

---

[63] Ibid., 784.
[64] Ibid., 765.
[65] The critic W.D. Howarth goes so far as to classify the play as a *pièce à thèse* in his *Sublime and Grotesque: a study of French Romantic drama* (London: Harrap, 1975). For his discussion of *Chatterton*, see pp.263–7.
[66] Vigny, I, 767.

ker who, here too, plays a mediating role, scolds Chatterton: 'En toi, la rêverie continuelle a tué l'action', he says, but Chatterton counters, 'Eh! qu'importe, si une heure de cette rêverie produite plus d'œuvres que vingt jours de l'action des autres? Qui peut juger entre eux et moi?'[67]

Though drawn back into society by the inescapable needs of his body and the unavoidable participation in the market economy, Chatterton dreams of a role for the poet on the margins of society, as a kind of priest or Moses figure.[68] His duty is to: 'Réveiller de froides cendres, quand tout frémit et souffre autour de moi ... quand l'Espérance a perdu son ancre; la Foi, son calice ... quand la Loi est athée et corrompue comme une courtisane; lorsque la Terre crie et demande justice au Poète de ceux qui la fouillent sans cesse pour avoir son or, et lui disent qu'elle peut se passer du Ciel.'[69] Poetry does not have a use value but represents a value outside of the capitalist system, and might be understood in terms of the Bataillan concept of expenditure. In his well-known article 'La Notion de dépense' Georges Bataille provides a critique of traditional Western economic theories, which subordinate the idea of expenditure to the idea of utility, seen as the main purpose of economic intercourse. He argues that in cultures in which gift exchanges or *potlach* are required, a notion of expenditure or of loss (*perte*) is valorised above the mercantile notions of acquisition and conservation of goods. Seen this way, poetry and the endeavour of the poet can be considered a kind of expenditure or *potlach*, superfluous to the physical needs of society, but nevertheless fulfilling a spiritual function in the values of the culture. Chatterton, however, does not live in such a culture, and so his sacrifice is unrecognised and inefficacious. His is the bourgeois culture, condemned by Bataille as having imposed 'la mesquinerie universelle'[70] by squelching expenditure. John Bell represents the bourgeoisie, for whom, according to Bataille, 'les

---

[67] Ibid., 772.
[68] See also Vigny's 'Moïse', in Poèmes antiques et modernes, Œuvres complètes, I.
[69] Vigny, I, 794.
[70] Georges Bataille, *Œuvres complètes, Premiers Écrits (1922–1940)* (Paris: Gallimard, 1970), 314.

The Limits of Performance in the French Romantic Theatre   47

processus d'échange ont un sens acquisitif',[71] since, different from the aristocracy, the bourgeoisie 'n'a consenti à *dépenser* que *pour soi*'.[72] Chatterton is trapped in this closed system whose basic principles are utility and conservation; as poet, he represents the potential for an opening up of the system onto a higher law, but his promise will never be realised.

It is tempting to read Chatterton's suicide as *potlach*, but an examination of the circumstances of the poet's death precludes that interpretation. After the Act III, scene ii soliloquy in which Chatterton expounds on the duties of the poet and then resolves to commit suicide, the Quaker, realising the danger Chatterton is in, exhorts him to think of Kitty Bell. He reveals Kitty's love for Chatterton and warns him that if he dies, Kitty will die as well. Chatterton's *crie de cœur* echoes Antony's, when he exclaims: 'Hélas! je ne puis donc plus vivre ni mourir?'[73] He resolves to try to live in society, to accept whatever aid the Lord Maire offers him and to forget about poetry. In Act III, scene vi, for the first time, we see Chatterton playing a role, as he pretends to be grateful and submissive to his noble protector. He steels himself to the task, saying, 'Pour elle! pour elle! je boirai le calice jusqu'à la lie'.[74] But the performance is impossible to sustain. Left alone, Chatterton begins to burn his poetry, as a sacrifice to Kitty Bell, but when he learns in quick succession that the Lord Maire's generosity consists of an offer to employ him as valet and that he has been accused in the press of plagiarising his poems, he drinks a vial of opium, saying, 'Ô mon âme, je t'avais vendue! je te rachète avec ceci.'[75] Now, as he continues to burn his papers, it is in the old mode of protecting them from the incomprehension of the world. 'Allez, nobles pensées écrites pour tous ces ingrats dédaigneux, purifiez-vous dans la flamme et remontez au ciel avec moi!'[76]

At this point, Kitty Bell enters and in Act III, scene viii, they share their only *tête-à-tête* of the play. In this scene, they finally admit their

[71]   Ibid., 311.
[72]   Ibid., 313.
[73]   Vigny, I, 798.
[74]   Ibid., 806.
[75]   Ibid., 809.
[76]   Ibid., 810.

love for one another, but it is too late. Chatterton has already drunk the poison; he is already dead. He attempts to separate himself from her, to disentangle their fates, claiming for himself the glory of a sacrificial suicide, and in climbing the stairs to his room, a sort of symbolic apotheosis of the poet. While we the audience can see Chatterton's death in this light, we already know that society will see it differently. He may die for the sake of the purity of his art, but his body, as we have already learned, will be reintegrated into the system of exchange as the means by which his debts will be paid. Chatterton's death is, in this way, the opposite of *potlach*, since it serves a specific use function. It is Kitty's death, which follows Chatterton's immediately, that can and must be read as *potlach*. Nothing useful can be made of her death, nor can the closed system of the bourgeois culture make sense of her dying for a lover to whom she has barely ever spoken. Rather, Kitty's dead body substantiates the higher law by which Chatterton had tried to live. In the end, it is Kitty's body that stands as proof of the higher value of the poet, of the purity of his endeavour and the power of his love.

Conclusions

As in *Un Caprice* and *La Quenouille de Barbérine*, in *Antony* and *Chatterton*, performance points to a deeper real. In the plays we discussed in Part One, society has it right, and the work of performance in the play is to normalise those who would transgress the value of fidelity. In the plays we discussed in Part Three, society has it wrong, and the work of the play is to create through performance a new society, attuned to the higher values of true love and pure art. In the plays we looked at in Part Two, however, a question about whether there is any mooring at all to society's values persists; performance in these plays forces us to confront an uneasy proof, which is always shifting, but tends to settle with power, rather than with a set of values.

In all six plays, meaning is at least temporarily unstable. It is through performance that meaning is stabilised, leaving the audience affirmed in their beliefs, diverted and satisfied, as in *Un Caprice* and *La Quenouille de Barbérine*; or through performance, a higher meaning is indicated, leaving the audience saddened but aware of belonging to something larger than themselves, as in *Antony* and *Chatterton*; or as in *Quitte pour la peur* and *Kean,* performance allows meaning to be absconded with, leaving the audience at a loss. In every case, though, abstract meaning is tied to something or someplace physical: in Chavigny's purse or in the thread Rosemberg spins; hidden in the bedroom of La Duchesse or far away in New York; in Adèle's or Kitty's dead body. Whether the play highlights the gap between the abstract and the concrete, or abolishes it temporarily, the structure of theatre is such that it cannot but comment on the distance between our world as it is and our world as idealised on the stage.

Chapter II: Resistance

In our Chapter One discussion of performance and proof, we saw how performances within plays are often aimed at arriving at some physical substantiation of an abstract value. A successful performance leaves the characters and, by extension, the audience, reaffirmed in some preexisting belief shared by the community; the failure of performance can leave an open question about the values a community is supposed to share; a third type of performance substantiates the values not of the community as a whole but of some happy few, who find themselves constituted as community in their shared understanding of a better value, misunderstood by the community at large. In this chapter, through readings of three plays by Victor Hugo (1802–1885), we will explore at greater length the constitution of community through performance and the role of the individual in the process.

Pierre Barbéris, among many others, argues that the young men writing around 1830 are confronting feelings of disillusionment as the Revolution of 1789, which was supposed to guarantee that people had 'la possibilité d'être heureux, de s'accomplir, de se réaliser, les obstacles dressés par les nobles, les rois et les prêtres étant à jamais brisés',[1] led instead only to the new reign of money. According to Barbéris the struggles of the young men who found themselves excluded from the power structures of the Restoration gave rise to a new literary model: 'Contre [les hommes d'argent] apparaît un type nouveau de héros: le jeune homme pauvre, porteur de valeurs, brimé, non par la naissance et les souvenirs d'ancien régime, mais bien par ce qu'il y a de plus virulent, de plus fort dans le monde moderne: l'argent'.[2]

---

[1] Pierre Barbéris, 'Structures et dynamiques du romantisme', in *Manuel d'histoire littéraire de la France*, Pierre Abraham (éd.) (Paris: Éditions sociales, 1972), IV, 478.
[2] Pierre Barbéris, 'Le Romantisme plébéien', ibid., IV, 512–3.

Barbéris's argument and traditional scholarship on Romanticism agree that the central theme of Romantic theatre is the young man's conflict with his society, his quest to establish his own place in history. In fact, the trajectory which Barbéris traces for the romantic hero — expulsion from society, conflict, and finally reintegration or death — follows Victor Turner's 'social drama' structure, outlined in the introduction to this volume. But while Barbéris's description is certainly apt, it elides questions about subjectivity and collectivity and simplifies the conflict to one between two clearly-defined adversaries. I will argue, rather, following René Girard, Georges Bataille and Victor Turner, that communities define themselves in conflict, through the recognition and exclusion of alterity. Moreover, they are never so secure in their ideals that they can forego the quest for substantiation of their values in conflict; in other words, they seek out conflict as a means of substantiating the abstract claims they make in their self-definition. At the same time, the excluded individual comes to define himself and his values in opposition to the community that has rejected him. We might go so far as to say that in the Romantic theatre, the hero actually comes to exist as subject through this violent rupture with his community. The hero's successful integration would reorder the society, but as we will see, for the heroes of Victor Hugo's plays, three of which we will discuss in the present chapter, integration is always temporary and leads not to a coherent subjectivity but to fracture, loss and death.

Hugo's aesthetic, which he enunciates most clearly in the preface to the 1827 historical drama *Cromwell*, rests on the foundation of duality. Hugo is writing during the heat of the battle over dramatic reform and the purpose of his preface is to demonstrate that the *drame* — and not tragedy — is the dramatic form best able to express the contemporary real. He argues that the grotesque (which he defines as the juxtaposition of comic and tragic elements, high and low language, etc.) represents the modern ideal of art, since it is a more faithful mimesis of nature than the classical aesthetic, which represents only the beautiful. According to Hugo, the need for the grotesque in art is specifically Christian, for just as Christ allies divinity and humanity, the grotesque mixes the beautiful and the ugly, the tragic and the comic. Since Christianity is double, the real is doubled and thus the grotesque becomes the key to the representation of the real. Indeed, doubles abound in the dramaturgy of Hugo, but while the preface to *Cromwell* implies that the double is the means to truth or transcendence, in *Hernani, Ruy Blas,* and *Le Roi s'amuse*, the final result is rupture.

In her seminal book on Hugo, *Le Roi et le bouffon*, Anne Ubersfeld deals at length with the problem of the fractured subject in Hugo's theatre. She suggests a biographical source for the conflict in Hugo's relationship with his parents. His father had fought for the Revolution and was later a general under Napoleon; his mother was a *vendéenne* who believed to the last in the divine right of kings. The two were in perpetual conflict and young Victor Hugo apparently never enjoyed the presence of one parent without suffering from the absence of the other.[3] Ubersfeld argues:

> Le moi hugolien est celui qui doit et ne peut réconcilier en lui 'mon père, vieux soldat, ma mère vendéenne'. La mise en question du père et de la mère ne peut se comprendre indépendamment des instances historiques. La rupture avec le père, c'est aussi la chute de l'Empire. La liquidiation du souvenir de la mère, c'est aussi la chute de la monarchie absolue.[4]

Indeed, Hugo's literary career, which began in 1819 when he founded the literary journal *Le Conservateur Littéraire* with his brothers, was always narrowly associated with politics. He went on to become an important advocate for the Romantic school in poetry, the novel and particularly in the theatre where there was an overtly political battle to be fought. Later, after the 1848 revolution, Hugo served in the legislature but was exiled by Napoleon III in 1852. After 1870 he returned to France and continued both his literary and political careers. When he died in 1885, he was recognised as the most influential French author of the nineteenth century.

Politics, the law and history are always important in Hugo's plays, as they were in his life. We have talked about the 1830s as a transitional moment in French politics and significantly Hugo often chooses to stage transitional moments in his plays, moments when a new regime comes

---

[3] Anne Ubersfeld, *Le Roi et le bouffon* (Paris: José Corti, 1974), 18. Ubersfeld cites the unpublished text of *Victor Hugo raconté* to support this claim.
[4] Ibid., 19.

into conflict with an old law. For example, the plots of all of the plays we will discuss in this chapter are powered by vengeance. As early as Aeschylus' *Eumenides*, it has been argued that the natural law of vengeance is replaced, as civilisation develops, by the foundation of the judiciary. While *Hernani, Ruy Blas* and *Le Roi s'amuse* all theoretically take place in juridical cultures, Hugo places his characters, as we have already noted, deliberately outside of society, and therefore beyond the reach of society's remedies. The older law of vengeance draws the heroes back to an earlier order to which they do have access. In a movement of ambivalent nostalgia, the heroes are propelled forward by their desire to integrate into society and at the same time pulled backwards by their own past. Ultimately, they are all destroyed and, as Ubersfeld puts it, '... le drame de Hugo est vécu comme l'impossibilité de réparer, de combler la faille intérieure'.[5] What we have to find out in exploring the conflict between the individual and his community is whether that destruction is meaningless carnage which produces only despair, or whether it can produce meaning and lead to the possibility of transcendence, if not for the individual, for a community reconstituted by the proximity of death.

Part One. Performance and Discontinuity in Hernani

When *Hernani* was first produced on 25 February 1830, at the Comédie Française, the conflict over dramatic reform was at boiling point. Partisans of the young author packed the theatre early and intended to cheer the play on to a successful run.[6] But partisans of the classicists were present, too, and they vowed to boo the play into submission. Throughout the performance many lines were, indeed, jeered at, but the king's long soliloquy in Act IV won the crowd over and the performance of Mlle Mars as Doña Sol in Act V brought the house down. *Hernani* was savaged in the press, but went on to nearly fifty performances in its first run.

[5]   Ibid., 18.
[6]   During the nineteenth century, theatre owners and producers often employed workers known as 'la claque' to watch plays and applaud them, but *Hernani* was supported by an all-volunteer corps which included literary figures such as Gérard de Nerval, Théophile Gautier and Honoré de Balzac.

Hernani is the typical romantic hero we described in the introduction: in Spain in 1519, he finds himself excluded from his lands and titles because of the crimes of his father. He lives instead as chief of an outlaw band while plotting to avenge his father's execution at the hands of the late king by killing his son, the reigning king, Don Carlos. Hernani explains:

> Les pères ont lutté sans pitié, sans remords,
> Trente ans! Or, c'est en vain que les pères sont morts,
> Leur haine vit. Pour eux la paix n'est point venue,
> Car les fils sont aebout, et le duel continue. [7]

We are never told what caused the conflict between Hernani's father and the king, and it does not matter. The hero is compelled to complete his father's vengeance because it was his father's, and whether or not his father was in the right. This is the logic of vengeance as described by René Girard in *La Violence et le sacré*: 'La vengeance se veut représaille et toute représaille appelle de nouvelles représailles'.[8] At the same time that vengeance necessarily inscribes itself in a history of wrongs that have taken place; it need not have a long memory, since its grievance is always renewed by the latest reprisal. Driven forward by a quest for violence, Hernani is equally motivated by nostalgia for the lost father, whose quest it was originally.

In fact, the three main male characters are all driven by nostalgia. Don Carlos yearns after the glory years of the Holy Roman Empire in the long soliloquy in Act IV in which he addresses Charlemagne. And Don Ruy Gomez, who represents the old Spanish nobility and the laws of courtly honour, is ever evoking the days of yore, 'Quand nous avions le Cid et Bernard, ces géants / De l'Espagne et du monde …'.[9] If the three share a nostalgia which draws them backwards, towards their literal or spiritual fathers, they also share the goal that impels them forward, toward roman-

---

[7] Victor Hugo, *Théâtre Complet* (Paris: Gallimard, 1962), I, 1164.
[8] René Girard, *La Violence et le sacré* (Paris: Grasset, 1972), 28.
[9] Hugo, 1173.

tic love: each hopes to win the love of Doña Sol, the niece and fiancée of the elderly Don Ruy Gomez.[10]

We can draw a parallel between the characters' conflicting impulses in *Hernani* and the double movement of the erotic experience as described by Georges Bataille in *L'Érotisme*. For Bataille, the essential state of a person is 'discontinuity': 'Entre un être et un autre, il y a un abîme, il y a une discontinuité'. [11] The erotic impulse is related to an individual's need to make contact with an other, to overcome temporarily the discontinuity that defines our quotidian reality. Hernani's situation as an outlaw, banished from his society, certainly magnifies this condition, although Don Carlos and Don Ruy Gomez are both isolated as well: Don Carlos, by the singularity of kingship and Don Ruy Gomez in the decline of old age. Despite our discontinuity, however, Bataille argues that, thanks to our experience in the womb, we all have an instinct toward — what he calls a 'nostalgia' for — continuity with an other. 'Nous sommes des êtres discontinus', he writes, 'individus mourant isolément dans une aventure inintelligible, mais nous avons la nostalgie de la continuité perdue.'[12] Again, this loss of continuity is repeatedly enacted in *Hernani*, where each character is in turn ripped from Doña Sol: Hernani in Act I, Hernani and Don Carlos in Act II, Hernani and then Don Ruy Gomez in Act III, Don Ruy Gomez in Act IV and finally, Hernani and Don Ruy Gomez in Act V, as they both die with Doña Sol.

The impulse toward the other brought on by the nostalgia of continuity is for Bataille a kind of regression and represents a will to lose the self in, if not death (which happens literally in Act V of *Hernani*), its simulacrum. 'La reproduction mène à la discontinuité des êtres, mais elle met en jeu leur continuité, c'est-à-dire qu'elle est intimement liée à la mort.'[13] The erotic experience, the 'little death', is the closest approximation we have of the lost continuity we seek, and so the search for erotic union cannot be accomplished without violence. 'Essentiellement le domaine de

---

[10] An early proposed title for the play was, in fact, *Trois pour une* (Hugo, 1760).
[11] Georges Bataille, *L'érotisme* (Paris: Les Éditions de Minuit, 1957), 17.
[12] Bataille (1957), 20.
[13] Ibid., 17.

l'érotisme est le domaine de la violence, le domaine de la violation.'[14] In fact, each time Hernani and Doña Sol are together, they speak of death: for example, in Act I, Hernani imagines a future with Doña Sol in exile, 'Être errante avec moi, proscrite, et, s'il le faut, / Me suivre où je suivrai mon père, — à l'échafaud.'[15] Even at the beginning of Act V, when on their wedding night they are preparing to go to bed, Doña Sol exclaims, 'Et j'aurais bien voulu mourir en ce moment!'[16]

The erotic experience as described by Bataille is thus related to notions of communication and of death. According to Bataille, 'nulle communication entre nous ne pourra supprimer une différence première. Si vous mourez, ce n'est pas moi qui meurs.'[17] We cannot suppress the abyss of death that separates us, nor can we communicate across it; the most we can do, says Bataille is 'en commun ressentir le vertige de cet abîme'.[18] Erotic union is the experience in common of that abyss that comes with the temporary dissolution of the borders that define and separate each individual. Eroticism is about the reconfiguration of the individual and of his or her quotidian experience of reality. This is accomplished through an experience similar to that of death: the *expérience des limites* through which a person feels, paradoxically, the discontinuity of his or her being in its most potent form: the transgression of the limits of the body in temporary *continuity* with an other. 'Toute la mise en œuvre de l'érotisme a pour fin d'atteindre l'être au plus intime, au point où le cœur manque.'[19] This violent shock of realities, this reconfiguration of the individual is the abstract violence of which Bataille speaks and it encompasses much more than the individual in its scope. 'Ce qui est en jeu dans l'érotisme est toujours une dissolution des formes constituées. [...] de ces formes de vie sociale, régulière, qui fondent l'ordre discontinu des individualités définies que nous sommes.'[20] We can argue that the *expérience des limites*

[14] Ibid., 21.
[15] Hugo, 1166.
[16] Ibid., 1300.
[17] Bataille (1957), 17.
[18] Ibid., 17.
[19] Ibid., 22.
[20] Ibid., 23.

described by Bataille is an example of what Victor Turner calls 'liminality', or at least that they are related concepts. Turner describes 'the limen, or threshold' as 'a no-man's-land betwixt-and-between the structural past and the structural future'.[21] Similarly, the *expérience des limites* is played out on the threshold which divides (and brings together) eroticism and death, self and other. Most significantly, for both Turner and Bataille both the individual and the community will be restructured by the liminal experience.

The *expérience des limites* is staged in the first act of the play, when Don Carlos and Hernani are separately introduced to Doña Sol's bedchamber under cover of night. Don Carlos tells us, moreover, that Hernani's visits to Doña Sol have been going on for some time. 'La belle adore / Un cavalier sans barbe et sans moustache encore, / Et reçoit tous les soirs, malgré les envieux / Le jeune amant sans barbe à la barbe du vieux.'[22] Later, the two men will fight, introducing literal violence and the real possibility of death into a situation in which violence was up to that point figured only linguistically, as we saw earlier, and symbolically (by the scaling of walls and climbing of hidden staircases). In Act II, as she struggles against Don Carlos, Doña Sol takes his dagger and subsequently the dagger will appear in every meeting between Doña Sol and Hernani. The presence of the dagger represents several things: first, it is the symbol of Doña Sol's fidelity. Armed with the dagger, she can resist her other suitors and she need only show Hernani the dagger in Act III, scene iv and Act IV, scene iv to prove to him that she has remained faithful. Moreover, the dagger, in all its phallic potential, itself represents the violence and danger inherent in the erotic experience, while Doña Sol's possession of it represents the reconstitution of the individual in the erotic experience, as she takes on a characteristic of the masculine order. Finally, her failure to use the dagger to protect Hernani against the resurgent Don Ruy Gomez in Act V, scene vi, re-inscribes her in the feminine order, evacuating the erotic tension of the scene, as, throwing the dagger, she exclaims, '… Monseigneur, je ne suis qu'une femme'.[23]

[21] Turner, 11.
[22] Hugo, 1156.
[23] Ibid., 1311.

Nor is Doña Sol alone reconfigured by the erotic experience. In each possible coupling of Doña Sol with one of her suitors, there are potential ramifications in the social order and in the social position of the individuals involved. For Don Carlos, a merely sexual union with Doña Sol would have no effect on his status, although it would obviously consign her to a *demi-monde*, outside the sphere of respectability to which she was born: 'Moi je suis fille noble, et de ce sang jalouse, / Trop pour la concubine, et trop peu pour l'épouse.'[24] As she resists him, Don Carlos ponders what could be done for him to have her. The only possibility is to reconfigure the social order by fiat and so he offers her a share in his social status: 'Eh bien, partagez donc et mon trône et mon nom. / Venez. Vous serez reine, impératrice!'[25] We know that Don Carlos has the power to affect such a change in the social order, for we see on two different occasions that with a word (and an unintentional word, at that) he promotes one of his courtiers to count in Act II, scene i and then to 'Grand d'Espagne' in Act IV, scene i. It would seem, then, that the king's word really is law and the king's violent desire for Doña Sol threatens the very order from which his power emanates.

In the proposed marriage between Doña Sol and Don Ruy Gomez there is, at first, no question of the erotic reconfiguration of the social order, for their union is based on family honour and not on personal desire. Moreover, as Doña Sol tells Hernani in Act I, 'Le roi, dit-on, le veut ...'.[26] We have seen that when the king's will changes, the social order changes with it, but Don Ruy Gomez is subject to a law greater than the law of the king's whim, and in standing firm in his old traditions, ironically becomes a threat to the tenuous social order. His fall from grace occurs in Act III, when Don Carlos demands Hernani's head. Don Ruy Gomez, who has unwittingly allowed Hernani sanctuary in his home, refuses to give him up since to do so would be to dishonour his family by breaking the law of hospitality. Don Carlos kidnaps Doña Sol in place of Hernani and Don Ruy Gomez finds himself outside of the dominant order for the first time. When, on becoming Holy Roman Emperor, Don Carlos renounces his

[24] Ibid., 1193.
[25] Ibid., 1194.
[26] Ibid., 1164.

own love for Doña Sol to offer her to Hernani, Don Ruy Gomez's love for Doña Sol remains a threat to the social order and will eventually destroy both the couple and himself in Act V. For Hernani, the outlaw, uniting with Doña Sol could not mean integration into society, as Doña Sol would lose her status in such a union; but their union outside of society might constitute an alternate community, based on the individual in love, rather than on family lineage, the past, or the king's will. Once Hernani is reinstated as Jean d'Aragon, on the other hand, union with Doña Sol is the apogee of his process of reintegration; only the return of Don Ruy Gomez can occasion his fall from such a height.

While for Bataille, erotic experience entails an *expérience des limites* – an experience of fusion with another body that forces us to experience intimately our own discontinuity from others in our quotidian world, it is, at the same time, an experience that forces us to recognise the 'limitation' of that quotidian configuration by placing it temporarily into question. Death is engaged because it is at least symbolically what is 'at stake' in the dissolution of the individual in the erotic experience. When Don Carlos unites Hernani and Doña Sol, Hernani undergoes a symbolic death, as he loses the identity of Hernani and everything associated with it — exile, vengeance, lawlessness — to become Jean d'Aragon, landed, at peace, integrated into the society. Their love is now (as was the case with the couple Don Ruy Gomez / Doña Sol at the opening of the play) entirely sanctioned and so there is no further need to scale walls or draw swords: the erotic tension is thus fairly drained from their relationship, if not from the play. If Don Carlos has found a kind of continuity in his role as emperor (like Hernani, he changes his name to mark the transformation), if his place in history as heir to Charlemagne allows him to renounce his claims on Doña Sol, and if Hernani has become through Doña Sol and the intervention of the king a part of the whole of society, an integrated subject (subject, too, to the king's law), Don Ruy Gomez remains still the same, frustrated, discontinuous outsider he became when Don Carlos took Doña Sol away from him in Act III. It is the violent expression of his rage that finally unites Don Ruy Gomez not so much to Doña Sol, but to Hernani, whose death he calls for in Act V.

We have seen that the erotic moves in two directions: backwards in nostalgia toward the original continuity and forward, toward death.

Moreover, we have argued that vengeance works in the same way; moving backwards in that it responds to some earlier crime and forward, toward the death of the other, which is also potentially the death of the self. In Act V of *Hernani,* Don Ruy Gomez's vengeance against the young hero, linked to Hernani's original vengeance quest by the oath on his father's head in Act III, scene vii, will break into the erotic just when the erotic has lost its violent impulse. Doña Sol describes her temporary, total continuity with Hernani thus:

> ... Mon duc rien qu'un moment!
> Le temps de respirer et de voir seulement.
> Tout s'est éteint, flambeaux et musique de fête.
> Rien que la nuit et nous. Félicité parfaite.[27]

The lovers are alone together in a dark and silent place, but their 'perfect felicity' can last only a moment. Doña Sol represents for Hernani the maternal, the feminine, the origin of his being, but when Don Ruy Gomez enters (and we first hear the horn only four speeches after the moment described above), he comes embodying the opposite principle, the law of the fathers, to enforce his vengeance, to reinforce Hernani's belonging to the masculine order and to re-establish his discontinuity.

The final scene of *Hernani* is striking in its reversal of the play's earlier logic. Doña Sol, who represented the dream of continuity for all three of the male protagonists earlier in the play, is here excluded from the intercourse between Hernani and Don Ruy Gomez. Throughout the scene, she tries to interrupt them, but they talk right over her, as if she were not even there.

> DOÑA SOL
> Un instant! voilà tout, tout ce que je réclame! --
> Enfin on laisse dire à cette pauvre femme
> Ce qu'elle a dans le cœur! ... — Oh! laissez-moi parler!

---

[27] Ibid., 1300. We will see a similar momentary integration when Lorenzo de Medicis finally assassinates the Duc in Musset's *Lorenzaccio.* See our discussion of this play in Chapter Three.

DON RUY GOMEZ, à *Hernani.*
J'ai hâte.

When Doña Sol grabs the vial of poison from Hernani, Don Ruy Gomez, who had up to this point reminded Hernani of his filial obligation to keep the promise made on his father's head, becomes more blunt. 'Puisque je n'ai céans affaire qu'à deux femmes, / Don Juan, il faut qu'ailleurs j'aille chercher des âmes',[28] he tells Hernani, derisively categorising the young hero as a woman, like Doña Sol, who cannot belong to the masculine order he represents. It is at this point, as Don Ruy Gomez moves to leave, that Hernani distinguishes himself from Doña Sol and demands that she give him back the poison. Hernani has chosen with the father(s), to belong to the order of the promise, the order of the word.

But Doña Sol is not without agency. Before giving the vial to Hernani, she drinks half of it herself, reinforcing in the death they will share a physical connection, deeper than the filial relationship Hernani is trying to salvage between himself and his dead father through the surrogacy of his promise to Don Ruy Gomez. Finally, it seems as if in death, Hernani will experience continuity without compromise: his suicide links him with the law of the father and at the same time, dying with Doña Sol, he will be connected to the body of the mother. W.D. Howarth argues that this scene plays out 'the supreme Romantic myth of twin souls finding perfect communion in a shared, unblemished love', a desire which, 'perhaps necessarily carries with it a death wish'.[29] On one level Howarth is correct, and yet, a careful examination of the death scene uncovers a troubling incongruity. Doña Sol drinks her half of the poison first but her death is slower and much more painful than his: '... Est-ce pas qu'on souffre horriblement?' she asks; 'Non' is the hero's reply.[30] While their death, which at first glance represents the ultimate romantic / erotic union of the lovers, the *mise en scène* of their utter continuity reveals instead the underlying logic of discontinuity that Bataille describes. Their attempts at

---

[28] Hugo, 1314.
[29] W.D. Howarth, *Sublime and Grotesque: a study of French Romantic drama* (London: Harrap, 1975), 169.
[30] Hugo, 1317.

the *expérience des limites* are meant to conceal the final, essential truth of being: 'Si vous mourez, ce n'est pas moi qui meurs.'[31] The death of Hernani and Doña Sol enacts that discontinuity by revealing to what extent two lovers sharing the same death still die alone, for while Doña Sol dies for love in a last attempt to be as one with Hernani, the hero dies for honour, because he must prove that he is worthy not of Doña Sol, but of his father.

We have cast the final scene as a conflict between the male and female principles: the body-love of the mother and the word-law of the father. But what of the law of the emperor? Why is his law, dictated to him in the tomb by Charlemagne himself, powerless over the vengeance of Don Ruy Gomez? Despite the discourse in the tomb about the elected status of 'Ces deux moitiés de Dieu, le pape et l'empereur',[32] which gives them supremacy over the kings who are born to their position, and despite what we know to be true about Hugo's increasingly republican political beliefs,[33] the law that functions here finds its origin in a much deeper past than any of the individuals in the story – including ninth-century Charlemagne. This play is on the political level a story about establishment, the establishment of Charles V and the ascendancy of Spain on the world stage; it is the story of the displacement of the old law of vengeance, replaced with clemency. But the final act (in which, significantly, Charles V does not appear) shows the powerlessness of political forms, of 'society' to reproduce themselves without violence; just as the love plot shows the powerlessness of social forms such as marriage to contain the erotic experience without violence.

Vengeance, which comes back like a bad dream in the form of Don Ruy Gomez in Act V, is the return of the 'violence intestine' which the sacrifice is supposed to assuage and the judiciary is supposed to control.

---

[31] Bataille (1957), 17.
[32] Hugo, 1263.
[33] When Hugo wrote *Hernani* he was still fuming over the interdiction of *Marion de Lorme*, that was to be performed at the Comédie Française in 1829. *Hernani* is much more overtly political; although the foreign setting may have helped to allay the nerves of the ruling party who felt that *Marion de Lorme* made light of the 'personne royale' (Ubersfeld (1993), 102, 103).

Girard argues that violence is unavoidable in human interaction and that vengeance is particularly dangerous to society because 'La seule vengeance satisfaisante, devant le sang versé, consiste à verser le sang du criminel...'[34] Society cannot allow violence to run out of control in the infinite spiral of reprisals occasioned by vengeance, and so gives violence a sacred function in the sacrifice or takes over the function of vengeance in the judiciary. In *Hernani*, Don Carlos, in his first act as Charles V, eschews vengeance against his conspirators, in favour of the clemency dictated by Charlemagne, hoping to end the cycle there. Somehow, though, violence manages to erupt, like the return of the repressed, because its roots go deeper than society itself. The foundational moment of all society is a moment of exclusion when the society constitutes itself by expelling or eliminating an other, and whose alterity allows the society a vocabulary in which to define itself. Similarly, the act of being born (the first experience of discontinuity) is an expulsion that marks the difference between self and other. That societies and individuals need to re-enact this drama of foundation (and that Hugo stages it within a drama of political foundation) is an example of the parallel between the drive to commit vengeance and the desire toward the erotic *expérience des limites*, both of which play precisely on the border between life and death, self and other, profane and sacred. *Hernani* is itself staged on this border and reveals ultimately the powerlessness not of the individual in conflict with his society or the individual excluded from history but of the society in conflict with its own repressed desires and of the society detached from its origins.

Part Two. Time and Stage in Ruy Blas

Frustrated with ongoing resistance from the Comédie Française and the official theatre world, but still desirous of a level of respectability denied the boulevard theatres, Hugo, along with Alexandre Dumas and Casimir Delavigne, sought and received permission from the Duc d'Orléans to found their own theatre in 1836. This Second Théâtre Français – a name

---

[34] Girard, 28.

later rejected in favour of Théâtre de la Renaissance – would be another national stage where the *drame* would be at home. It did not, however, receive any government subsidies, but rather was funded by a private individual, an ex-vaudevillian who had made some money in business. Though according to their agreement with the sponsor the *drames* of Dumas and Hugo would now share the stage with light opera and vaudeville, the dramatists had a degree of artistic control at the Théâtre de la Renaissance that they had not previously experienced. Their rivalry was kept more or less in check by the director of the theatre, their mutual friend Anténor Joly.[35]

The play that inaugurated the new theatre in 1838 was Hugo's *Ruy Blas*, starring Frédérick-Lemaître in the title role. The play had a successful run, but like *Hernani*, negative reviews; it would seem that the change of stage had done nothing for Hugo's credibility as playwright. Gustave Planche, who could always be counted on to pan any Romantic *drame*, wrote in *La Revue des deux mondes* that the period sets and costumes overpowered the characters, that Hugo had managed to 'confondre l'homme et la chose, la vie et la pierre, le cœur et l'étoffe'.[36] This is not too far from George Steiner's estimation in 1961. He writes: 'What makes of [Hugo's] plays such vehement trivialities? Surely, the reason is that in them the theatre triumphs so relentlessly over the drama'.[37] About *Ruy Blas* in particular he adds: 'Splendid, in its own special way, but completely hollow to any touch of intelligence. The shapes of drama are being evoked without the substance.'[38] What these critics — separated by more than a century, but joined by an unbroken chain of critics who repeat the same condemnation of Hugo's plays — despise in Hugo is a lack of psychological depth to the characters. While they are not wrong – Hugo is no Shakespeare – they fail to appreciate *Ruy Blas* for what it is: an examination of the prison of social convention through the medium

---

[35] For more on the history of the Théâtre de la Renaissance, see Ubersfeld (1994), 143–4 and *Le Théâtre en France*, ed. Jacqueline de Jomarand (Paris: Armand Colin, 1992), 582–3.
[36] Cited in Ubersfeld (1993), 21.
[37] George Steiner, *The Death of Tragedy* (New York: Faber and Faber, 1961), 161.
[38] Ibid., 163.

and the metaphor of stage convention. Ruy Blas is not whole: how can he be when he is trapped by obscure birth in the costume of a valet, which does not accord with the elevation of his soul? On seeing him in his livery, his old friend Don César (himself playing the role of the bandit Zafari) asks if it is a disguise. Ruy Blas replies sadly, 'Non, je suis déguisé quand je suis autrement.'[39] So it is through performance that he will attempt to find coherence, to bring into harmony his world and his inner life. But Ruy Blas finds that he is equally trapped by the conventions of the stage, that he must obey the director and the logic of the plot. When his performance turns out to have been only a supporting role for a vengeance plot with which he wants nothing to do, he must reject performance, reject the temporary coherence he had felt while playing his role to become Ruy Blas again — out of place and most emphatically out of time.

Ruy Blas takes place in Spain in 1695 and closes a historical parenthesis about the grand period of Spanish history opened by *Hernani*. Like Hernani, Ruy Blas exists on the margins of society; but different from him, there is no pre-history that ordains that Ruy Blas 'really' belongs on the inside. Hernani is powered and eventually destroyed by that history and by his quest for vengeance. Ruy Blas, on the other hand, begins at an impasse – his love for the queen is impossible, given that he is just a valet and he can think of no way to make himself known to her – and he only moves forward under Don Salluste's power and under the name of his childhood friend and look-alike, Don César.[40] Eventually, both Hernani and Ruy Blas find themselves trapped by the immutable laws of their world; for Hernani, it is the law of the father and of vengeance, but in the case of Ruy Blas, those laws are no more or less than the conventions of the stage.

If Ruy Blas is merely a bit player in a larger *drame* over which he has no control, it is Don Salluste who conceives the vengeance plot, casts the

---

[39] Hugo, 1316.
[40] This dissolute nobleman, who leads an outlaw band under the name Zafari, is a comedic treatment of Hernani, for while Hernani struggles to find his place, Don César more or less happily cedes his place for five hundred ducats in Act I, scene ii.

parts, funds the production and in Act V, scene iii, calls for the curtain and prepares to take his bow. Throughout the play, the metaphor of theatre is foregrounded in the words and actions of the characters. In Act I, scene ii Don Salluste auditions his cousin Don César for the role of 'dashing young man who seduces the queen'. Don César remarks, 'D'honneur! vous avez l'air de faire un opéra. / Quelle part donnez-vous dans l'œuvre à mon génie?'[41] When Don César penetrates his cousin's intentions far enough to learn that he plans to seek vengeance against a woman he revolts and refuses to perform. Don César fails the audition, but must not know of Don Salluste's plan; so the old man deftly covers himself by congratulating his cousin on his high morals, explaining, 'Tout ce que j'ai dit là, c'est pour vous éprouver'.[42] In other words, to divert Don César's attention from the audition, Don Salluste calls attention to the audition structure and merely pretends that its content was different from what it was.

In need of a *jeune premier*, Don Salluste turns to his valet, who resembles Don César '... au point qu'on nous prenait / Pour frères'.[43] There is no need to bribe or cajole Ruy Blas, since he already works for the marquis. Ruy Blas will assume the identity of Don César, conveniently waylaid by the servants of Don Salluste so that he can pose no threat to the plot. Still, Don Salluste, like any good producer, has Ruy Blas sign a contract:

... Moi, Ruy Blas,
Laquais de Monseigneur le marquis de Finlas,
En toute occasion, ou secrète ou publique,
M'engage à le servir comme un bon domestique.[44]

He means to use this letter later, as he explains in Act III, scene v, as leverage, to keep Ruy Blas playing his role; for if he refuses to obey Don Salluste, he will send the letter revealing his true identity to the queen.

[41] Hugo, 1512.
[42] Ibid., 1514.
[43] Ibid., 1517.
[44] Ibid., 1528.

At first, Don Salluste does not need to pressure Ruy Blas at all. When Don Salluste tells him that his role is 'De plaire à cette femme et d'être son amant',[45] Ruy Blas is for the first time in a position, ironically thanks to his disguise, to express his true self. The servant and the master exchanging clothes is already, in 1838, a well-worn plot device in theatre. Hugo's critics are right here; he sacrifices verisimilitude for theatricality. By calling attention to the theatrical, however, Hugo is commenting on the absurdities of his contemporary society, where distinctions of birth, age and means keep commoners, young men and poor men from acceding to positions of importance. In Hugo's play, the lowborn Ruy Blas in the costume of Don César is a better Don César than the young nobleman ever was. He takes his responsibilities seriously; he governs wisely and fairly. In the six months that elapse between Act II and Act III, he has become, '... secrétaire / Universel, ministre, et puis duc d'Olmedo!'[46] Throughout the play, stage convention will amplify the absurdity of social convention.

Until he dons the clothes of Don César, the hero's only interaction with the queen had been as a secret admirer who scaled a garden wall each day to leave a certain flower on a bench for her to find. He does not know how touched the queen is by this attention, or how avid she is to learn the identity of her admirer. In their first scene together (Act II, scene iii), she puts together a series of clues and recognises Ruy Blas / Don César as her lover. At the same time, he discovers that the queen keeps '... Sur son cœur!'[47] a bit of lace torn from his sleeve and left behind with the flowers. Realising this, he nearly faints from delight and when he comes around, Ruy Blas says simply, '... Je renais! ...'.[48] While the queen represents all the possibilities of love and power to Ruy Blas (and indeed the ministers in Act III believe it is the queen who has promoted the interests of Don César), as it turns out, on the stage of Spain she is little more than a prop. In Act II, titled 'La Reine d'Espagne' we see the queen completely imprisoned by the arcane etiquette of the Spanish court. '... Il faut, pour que

---

[45] Ibid., 1535.
[46] Ibid., 1572.
[47] Ibid., 1558.
[48] Ibid., 1559.

la reine sorte', explains la Duchesse d'Albuquerque, 'Que chaque porte soit ouverte, — c'est réglé! — / Par un des grands d'Espagne ayant droit à la clé.'[49] All similar attempts to find amusement are thwarted in the same way, including the absurd pronouncement, '... Une reine d'Espagne / Ne doit pas regarder à la fenêtre.'[50] While earlier we argued that the foregrounding of theatricality introduces a social critique obliquely into the play, here, the staging of restrictive social convention presents a critique of the stage conventions of the classical and neoclassical theatre, in which numerous *bienséances*, or rules of good taste in language and action prevent the representation of anything deemed undignified.[51] The queen, who listens with pleasure to the song of the girls gathering lavender, is herself stuck in a world of stifling pretension, just as the élans of the Romantics are consistently criticised for being *de mauvais ton* at the Comédie Française.

From the time of his introduction to the queen in Act II until the return of Don Salluste in Act III, scene v, Ruy Blas climbs from obscurity to power, from loneliness to love. When the queen confesses her love for him in Act III, scene iii, Ruy Blas reaches the apogee of his journey. His soliloquy in Act III, scene iv opens with a visual metaphor: '...Devant mes yeux c'est le ciel que je voi!'[52] which is extended through the speech by the vocabulary of sight and light: 'rayons', 'cela m'éblouit', 'je regardais', 'je crois la voir encor'. The visual is essential to Ruy Blas for whom the outside appearance (the livery of a lackey) used to be at variance with inner reality (his noble soul). Now, for the first time Ruy Blas approaches psychological wholeness because outer appearances, inner desires and external reality are all in accord. 'Partout en moi, hors moi, joie, extase, mystère ...' and later, 'Cet ange, qu'à genoux je contemple et je nomme, / D'un mot me transfigure et me fait plus qu'un homme.'[53] Of

---

[49] Ibid., 1541.
[50] Ibid., 1547.
[51] The classic example of *bienséances* run amok is the refusal of the Comédie Française to permit the lowly but indispensable word 'mouchoir' (handkerchief) in the 1792 translation of *Othello* by Jean-François Ducis.
[52] Hugo, 1587.
[53] Ibid.

course, Ruy Blas is wrong, as Don Salluste's entrance confirms, but even before the return of the marquis, in that soliloquy of perfect happiness, Ruy Blas hints at what must, in the end, be his undoing. 'Duc d'Olmedo, — l'Espagne à mes pieds, — j'ai son cœur!' he cries, but Ruy Blas is not Duc d'Olmedo; Don César is. And if Ruy Blas has achieved a moment of bliss (or what we read as continuity in our discussion of *Hernani*), it can only be a moment. His happiness is only temporary because it is limited by the assumption of Don César's identity, limited by the rules of the play-within-the-play in which he does not have the starring role after all.

In *Le Roi et le bouffon*, Anne Ubersfeld reads the reversal of roles in *Ruy Blas* and other plays by Hugo, as an example of Bakhtine's 'littérature carnavalisée' in all the subversive potential of the carnival, which makes a fool a king and a king a fool. Bakhtine writes, 'C'est un jeu libre et joyeux, mais doté d'un sens profond. C'est le temps même qui en est le héros et l'auteur, le temps qui détrône, qui ridiculise et donne la mort à tout le vieux monde (le vieux pouvoir, la vieille vérité) pour donner en même temps naissance au nouveau'.[54] Certainly, as Ubersfeld notes, the charged political atmosphere of the 1830s, where kings are, in fact, collapsing all around is mirrored in the carnavelesque aspects of Hugo's *drames*. She characterises the action of Hugo's *drames* as 'intronisation / détronisation', a term taken from Bakhtine, which refers to the practice of creating out of a slave or a fool the king of carnival. This is certainly what happens in *Ruy Blas*, but as Bakhtine notes, 'L'intronisation contient déjà l'idée de la détronisation future: elle est ambivalente dès le départ'.[55] I am unconvinced that there is any ambivalence in the carnival as it is really practised, or that it has any subversive effect; however, it is certainly a staging of subversion, and like a play, is limited by the conventions which govern it and most importantly, as Bakhtine points out above, by time. Ubersfeld remarks that 'Le processus de

---

[54] Mikhaïl Bakhtine, *L'Œuvre de François Rabelais et la culture populaire au moyen âge et sous la renaissance*, tr. Andrée Robel (Paris: Gallimard, 1970), 208.
[55] Mikhaïl Bakhtine, *La Poétique de Dostoïevski* (Paris: Seuil, 1970–, cited in Ubersfeld (1974), 498.

carnavalisation suppose son propre point d'arrêt, le commandeur qui restaure l'ordre.'[56] In fact, when Don Salluste arrives in Act III, scene v, he is dressed as a lackey, completing the picture by taking the place of the servant, but he shows throughout the scene that it is he who has the real power. Don Salluste arrives just in time to say that time is up.

This project is about the effects and the limits of performance on our systems of belief, so I certainly would not want to reject Bakhtine's arguments out of hand. Carnival certainly fascinated many Romantic playwrights; indeed, two of Alfred de Musset's four most important plays take place during carnival. It is a period of licentiousness, of the world turned upside-down, and it seems replete with possibilities. In his article on Bakhtine, performance theorist Marvin Carlson focuses on those possibilities as he convincingly relates Bakhtine's concept of the 'carnivalesque' with Turner's 'liminality'.[57] I agree that what is enacted in a stage space (or in a carnival space) has subversive potential, but I believe that in the case of carnival that potential is always held in check by the structure of carnival itself; whereas the structure of theatre sometimes allows a certain subversive potential to realise itself because theatre remains open to interpretation. Richard Schechner describes the way in which at least contemporary carnival has been emptied out of its subversive potential by mediatisation, which '[knits] the many voices of the streets into a unitary broadcast'.[58] Schechner is certainly not wrong about the effects of the corporate-owned media on carnival and similar manifestations, but since carnival has always taken place with the sanction of and under the control of the structures of power, I am not convinced that carnival was ever really subversive, even before television. Likewise, the *intronisation* of Ruy Blas is never out of the control of Don Salluste.[59]

[56] Ubersfeld (1974), 505.
[57] Marvin Carlson, 'Theater and Dialogism' in *Critical Theory and Performance*, eds Janelle G. Reinelt and Joseph R. Roach (Ann Arbor: University of Michigan Press, 1992), 336–50.
[58] Richard Schechner, 'Invasions Friendly and Unfriendly: the dramaturgy of direct theatre' in ibid., 88–106 [105].
[59] As it happens, on the American Gulf Coast, carnival as it is practiced today is all about exclusion, secret societies, the continuation of a tradition of power and dominance by a certain group of people. It is, moreover, almost entirely racially

The marquis nearly loses control when the real Don César arrives inopportunely in Act IV in the apartment where the final act, Don Salluste's vengeance, is supposed to take place. He remarks immediately and repeatedly on the theatricality of the space in which he finds himself, 'Maison mystérieuse et propre aux tragédies. / Portes closes, volets barrés, un vrai cachot.'[60] Don César's predicament is indeed singular: he does not know where he is, exactly, but everyone who enters is looking for him, or at least for the person they think is Don César. The real Don César must play the part of Don César, even to the point of risking his life in a duel with Don Guritan, who believes him to be an imposter. Rather than upsetting Don Salluste's plot, however, Don César advances it further than even Ruy Blas, who, overwrought by the possibility that harm will come to the queen, has at this point abandoned his post. When Don Salluste enters, he reassures himself that his plan can still be executed and then has Don César arrested for his illegal activities as Zafari, the thief. Don Salluste thus clears the stage for *his* Don César by enforcing the assumed identity of the real Don César. Power sides with power, and the subversive potential of playacting is punished.

In the final act, however, there is time for one more reversal. Just as Don Salluste is about to force the queen to sign away her crown in an admission of adultery and to exile her — as she had exiled him before the play's opening — Ruy Blas stops acting. He refuses the names and titles the marquis offers him and cries out: 'Je m'appelle Ruy Blas, et je suis un laquais! / Ne signez pas, Madame! — Enfin! — Je suffoquais!'[61] He thus breaks Don Salluste's power — which depended on the threat to reveal his true identity — and stops performing. In doing so, he is sure to lose all possibility of a relationship with the queen, but he saves her honour. When he kills Don Salluste, over the objections of the queen, it is in part to protect her honour, but also to wipe out the origin of his false role. Still, Ruy Blas finds the future closed to him. Having experienced the power of a 'grand d'Espagne' and the love of the queen, he cannot go

segregated. My reading of Bakhtine is certainly colored by personal experience, as nothing could be less subversive than 'Mardi Gras' in Mobile, Alabama.
[60] Hugo, 1605.
[61] Ibid., 1652.

back to being a simple lackey, but he must go back to being Ruy Blas. His final act, after drinking poison himself, is to ask the queen to call him by his true name, and to love him in spite of who he is. The queen resists, but finally complies and in the last moment of the play, the story ceases to be about the vengeance of an old marquis and becomes a story of the recognition of lovers, who know each other in spite of external appearances.

Like Antony, Chatterton, Hernani and Lorenzo (whom we will discuss in Chapter Three), Ruy Blas has his time, his moment where appearance and inner reality come into accord and meaning centres on him, where coherence exists in and for him. But it is only temporary, for all these young men steal an hour or a moment from the present, which belongs to other forces. In his preface to *Ruy Blas*, Hugo offers a political reading of his play, explaining that Ruy Blas represents 'le peuple, qui a l'avenir et qui n'a pas le présent; le peuple, orphelin, pauvre, intelligent et fort; placé très bas, et aspirant très haut…'.[62] The theatre space is always the space of the present tense and yet *Ruy Blas* is about the impossibility of the present for the hero. For the present, he is only able to realise himself in the closed space of the theatre, in the limited time of the carnival, in the lifelike but unreal gesture of performance.

Part Three. Justice and Vengeance in Le Roi s'amuse

Triboulet, the hero of *Le Roi s'amuse,* is a professional performer and as with Dumas' *Kean,* the profession of the main character will occasion a further examination of the power and limitations of performance. We have already seen that Hernani and Ruy Blas are young men out of place and out of time, in conflict with an order that defines itself through conflict. Both characters fall victim to a vengeance which is not their own and which supersedes the political order to which they temporarily come to belong. *Le Roi s'amuse* is structurally almost the inversion: it is the hero Triboulet, the king's fool, who is the father figure and the hero who seeks vengeance. Moreover, unlike the other plays, the hero starts out more or less whole and is split apart over the course of the play by the

---

[62] Ibid., 1493.

loss of his daughter and his own quest for vengeance. In the first two plays a sort of justice prevails: Hernani obeys the law of the father and honours his word; Ruy Blas punishes Don Salluste and protects the queen. Their deaths, their bodies mean something in a system of values that inevitably crushes the individual under its weight. But there is no justice in *Le Roi s'amuse:* only the innocent dies and her body, which she willingly substitutes for the king's in a literal self-sacrifice, means nothing. It is perhaps the most cynical of all of Hugo's plays and, in my opinion, his greatest theatrical achievement.

First performed at the Comédie Française in 1832, *Le Roi s'amuse* enjoyed only one performance before its suspension and interdiction for immorality. Official censorship had been abolished in 1830, but Hugo's play, with its shocking representation of François I as a debauched rapist, was too strong to escape the notice of the government. Their interference, as it turns out, was probably unnecessary. The opening performance was not well received; giving reason to believe that the play's run would have been brief even without the ban. Hugo took the Comédie Française to court to argue for his play and though his defence of the freedom of the theatre was impassioned, it failed. *Le Roi s'amuse* was not performed again until 1882. Still the play served as the text for Verdi's 1851 opera *Rigoletto*, which was performed in Paris at the Théâtre-Italien in 1857 and, translated into French by Édouard Duprez, at the Théâtre-Lyrique in 1863. Through *Rigoletto, Le Roi s'amuse,* remains one of Hugo's best-known plays.

While Hernani and Ruy Blas consider themselves outcasts because of accidents of birth or fate, Triboulet's exclusion from full participation in society is not incidental but essential: he is deformed and his body puts him in the liminal position in which Kean found himself thanks to his talent. Both are admitted to the court and to high society for the amusement of others, but neither can ever really belong. Moreover, Triboulet's outward appearance does not correspond to his interior self. He is the king's fool by profession, but he is no fool, himself, and he shows repeatedly in scenes with the courtiers that he is their intellectual equal. Unlike Kean, however, who finds it impossible not to perform, Triboulet wants nothing more than to stop performing. He complains that even the most unfortunate of men has one thing he has not: 'Le droit de ne pas rire et de pleurer, s'il veut.'[63]

Still, Triboulet possesses a kind of functional — if limited — wholeness in his relationship with his daughter Blanche. Beautiful and pure, Blanche is everything Triboulet and his world are not and, with her, he feels complete. While the other heroes we have discussed are thwarted by fathers,[64] Triboulet finds in fatherhood that contingent wholeness that the other characters experience at different times: Ruy Blas while performing the duties of Don César, Hernani in love with Doña Sol. Triboulet tells Blanche that he wants nothing of the external world to enter their home; he even refuses to tell her his name, explaining:

> Je veux ici du moins, je veux en ta présence,
> Dans ce seul coin du monde où tout soit innocence,
> N'être pour toi qu'un père, un père vénéré,
> Quelque chose de saint, d'auguste et de sacré![65]

The purity of their home (figured, of course, in Blanche's virginity) is already threatened, though Triboulet does not yet know it, by the very king whose amorous adventures it is his job to encourage and by the jealous courtiers, eager to avenge themselves against the jests of the jester. Up to this point Triboulet has been able to negotiate the rupture between his external appearance and his internal self by keeping the two entirely separate. When his two worlds collide, he is confronted by the irreparable breach between his two equally real selves. His attempt, through vengeance, to repair his daughter's honour and regain his sense of wholeness will ultimately bring only chaos.

Traditionally the fool is an important character in Shakespearean theatre because in his wandering monologues he sometimes hits on a truth the other characters are unable to see or unwilling to speak. Triboulet is a

---

[63] Ibid., 1380.
[64] In Chapter One, we saw that Antony and Chatterton were undone rather by the absence of the father than by his presence. See also Chapter Three for a discussion of the complicated relationship of the hero to his various father figures in *Lorenzaccio*.
[65] Hugo, 1384.

different breed of fool – full of malice at his own deformity; he speaks maliciously to the courtiers, hinting at their wives' adultery and other familial disgraces to the pleasure of all but the target of the raillery. He speaks the truth, but not to power; François I is entirely spared the barbs of the fool, and he is likewise spared the anger of the husbands he has cuckolded. M. de Saint-Vallier, furious over the king's seduction of his daughter, Diane de Poitiers, is the only one to challenge the king's behaviour directly. After a long monologue about the crimes of the king against virtue, M. de Saint-Vallier curses both the king and Triboulet, who had mocked him. The force of the curse, however, falls entirely on Triboulet, the other father; far from being punished himself, the king becomes the instrument of Triboulet's punishment. This is true both of M. de Saint-Vallier's curse and the plot to abduct Blanche hatched by the courtiers. Triboulet has insulted them, but only François I is in a position to do them any real harm, and yet they avenge themselves only against the weaker party and use the stronger party as the means to accomplish it. Triboulet's vengeance is thus inscribed in the system of reprisals we mentioned earlier in our discussion of *Hernani*, but the reprisals are indirect or misdirected because they rarely take aim at the real wrong-doer and when they do, they fail to hit the mark: a substitute is always found.

Girard argues that, once awakened, violence will always find a way to satisfy itself, even if its real object is out of reach:

> La violence inassouvie cherche et finit toujours par trouver une victime de rechange. A la créature qui excitait sa fureur, elle en substitue soudain une autre qui n'a aucun titre particulier à s'attirer les foudres du violent, sinon qu'elle est vulnérable et qu'elle passe à sa portée.[66]

To most of the courtiers, avenging themselves against the king is entirely out of the question, as they have been paid in titles and honours for their cooperation with the king's erotic appetites, and as Triboulet charges in Act III, scene iii, they care more for their position than for the honour of sisters and wives. Only M. de Saint-Vallier and Triboulet, whose daughters were involved with — in the case of Blanche, raped by — François I,

---

[66] Girard, 11.

turn their anger directly on the king, the former because he believes himself to be the king's equal: 'Vous êtes roi, moi père, et l'âge vaut le trône'[67] and the latter because he is marginalised to the point where his reaction is not taken seriously. Triboulet's anger is surprising to the courtiers, but finally they respond with a sort of bemused indifference. 'Aux fous comme aux enfants on cède quelque chose',[68] explains M. de Gordes, as he and the other courtiers leave Triboulet and Blanche alone in the king's antechamber. No one expects Triboulet the fool to react as a father, and even were he to desire to avenge his daughter, the example of M. de Saint-Vallier, whom we see at the end of Act III being led to the Bastille for his strong words in Act I, would prevent any ordinary courtier, fearful for his place or even his life, from speaking up against the king.

We can see easily how and why the courtiers repress their anger with the king and turn it instead toward Triboulet in their plot to abduct Blanche, for they do not fear reprisal from the lowly fool. He is their scapegoat, tolerated among them at all so that he can serve that very function: as the weaker, uglier half of the king, he attracts all the anger and blame for the king's adulterous liaisons, while the king, charming, handsome and powerful, need accept only the glory and pleasure of the sexual conquest. The scapegoat belongs to the mode of sacrifice rather than the mode of vengeance because the function of the scapegoat is to be a victim who cannot be avenged, to halt the spiral of reprisals occasioned by vengeance. From the beginning, however, we are not in a purely sacrificial mode, as the scapegoat is not supposed to fight back. It is in this intermediate zone between vengeance and sacrifice that the anger of Triboulet misses its mark, destroying his own daughter in the place of the king. For though conceived and carried out by Triboulet as a vengeance, what was to be the king's death functions more like a sacrifice, with an innocent victim replacing the guilty party and with the witnesses to the event reconfigured as a community bound together by the father's loss.

[67] Hugo, 1371.
[68] Ibid., 1433.

As in *Hernani* and *Ruy Blas*, the society Hugo describes in *Le Roi s'amuse* is in transition, as the old values of honour and vengeance are beginning to make way for something new, consolidated royal power. We can see reflected in Hugo's staging of transitional moments the contemporary circumstances surrounding the creation of his plays. But these plays are all about more than a shift in the political system; they are about a shift in political and moral values and they question the very foundation of political and moral systems. In *Hernani*, the king's word was too weak to stop the old man's vengeance, but here, while Triboulet is working at vengeance, he is simultaneously undermined by Blanche and by the hired killers, Saltabadil and Maguelonne, who reroute vengeance toward a sacrificial function. For Saltabadil, violence is violence and the victim is irrelevant, as long as he gets paid. For Maguelonne and for Blanche, seduced by the charm of the young king, François I is worth saving and Blanche trades her own life for his, even knowing that he does not love her. In this way, Blanche allies herself with her lover / rapist instead of with her father. From the moment she was raped, Blanche had split from Triboulet, threatening his fragile self-definition. His vengeance is not just about Blanche's honour, but an attempt to remove François I who has become the obstacle to the paternal love for Blanche which gave his inner life structure and meaning. Since Blanche casts her lot with François I, however, Triboulet cannot help but destroy her with him and in the end destroy himself with her. The danger of vengeance is that it can spiral out of control and turn back on its doer: we have seen this in *Hernani* and *Ruy Blas*, where, as here, two conflicting moral codes are operative.

Still, if Blanche's death is supposed to be a sacrifice, as her final prayer makes explicit: 'J'offre pour un ingrat ma vie en sacrifice',[69] it is not particularly efficacious. The sacrifice is supposed to assuage violence and bind the community together in an understanding of their origins, the foundational act of violence that excluded the other and made them what they are. Here it tears everything apart and reveals the injustice at the base of the system: that power is the source of power, that François I can rape with impunity because he is François I. In the final scene, the com-

[69] Ibid., 1468.

munity does finally come around to sympathising with Triboulet's loss and in that way they are temporarily reconfigured. But François I goes off whistling a merry tune. He is still at large. The sexual danger he represents is untamed and, we may ask, how many sacrifices of young girls is it going to take to exorcise that threat? Repeated ones, for if we know anything about sacrifice, it is that it is already a re-enactment of a foundational moment and must be repeated periodically to assuage the doubts about values that arise sometimes in the form of violence within a community. Here, and we will discuss this further in the following chapter, theatre meets its ancestor the ritual sacrifice, as the repetition of the act of sacrificing the daughter exorcises some fear about virginity, sexual license and the place of the father in a world in transition.

Triboulet murders his daughter but he is no Agamemnon: the winds do not blow and no Klytemnestra will ever avenge Blanche. The play closes on Triboulet's despair at having sacrificed everything and come away with neither vengeance nor justice nor a meaningful sacrifice. The body of Blanche substantiates no collective, abstract idea, does not 'mean' anything to the father who lost her or to the witnesses who look on at his grief. Her body is only the troubling proof of her enduring love for the man who raped her, her total submission to power itself. This time, the law of the father is thwarted; the old law of vengeance is defeated by the son, the beautiful, charming, powerful young man. Love could not save Ruy Blas or Hernani, but the love of two women for whom he cares nothing saves François I without his even knowing it. He retains his position of privilege safe from the fathers who fade away unheeded with their old morals and defunct notions of honour.

Conclusions

We said it already: power sides with power in Hugo's theatre; the old men in the first two plays we talked about retain the power of the fading world and use it to destroy the sons. In *Le Roi s'amuse* the son is ascendant and uses his power to make the father irrelevant. This is the split in the subject Anne Ubersfeld talks about in her reading of Hugo's plays, only it is not mother and father, but father and son who cannot share the stage of history at the same time. Hugo is writing during a time of political, moral and theatrical transition, which rends the self, defines the times and destroys the nascent individual before he ever gets a chance to be. Hugo's theatre is about failure, but behind the failure there is a possibility, a hope that transcendent values exist and that the individual will one day come to be whole. Behind the masks of society, behind the blindness of hatred, behind the prejudice of class there is something real, a society that could be, which we glimpse for a moment with Doña Sol and Hernani, with the Queen and Ruy Blas, with Triboulet in his moment of bloody glory, a moment when right triumphs. But only a moment, limited to the time of performance, limited to the space of the stage.

Chapter III: Sacrifice

That the ancient tradition of the ritual sacrifice lies at the source of our theatre, that the stage writes over the palimpsest of the altar, has been a widely accepted theoretical position at least since Nietzsche. Stage and altar serve the same functions within a community and for an individual: they reify abstract ideas; they assemble a community as interpretive witness by re-enactment to truth, and they are the reminder of the structuring relationship of culture to the individual. What happens then, when, as in the three plays we will discuss in the present chapter, sacrifice no longer creates any transcendent meaning? What happens when performance fails to draw meaning from a visible referent or to confer meaning on an abstract idea? What happens when the subject forgets himself?

In Chapter Two we talked about plays by Hugo in which the heroes experience a limited moment of integration or of power but fail to find a place for themselves where they might be whole. Here, we will talk about plays by Musset in which the heroes rehearse different strategies, different *mises-en-scène* to realise their desires, but when reality falls short of fantasy, the result is more than a personal disappointment; it is a collective tragedy. As we mentioned in Chapter One, many of Musset's plays were not originally written for performance; in fact three of his four most important plays, those we will discuss in this chapter, were not performed in the author's lifetime. What accounts for the lasting resonance of this theatre, written ostensibly to be read and not performed? It is in part Musset's eagerness to eschew Hugolian symmetry and his willingness to explore a troubling and persistent gap between dream and reality. The characters in *Les Caprices de Marianne, On ne badine pas avec l'amour, Lorenzaccio,* and *Fantasio* — all written during Musset's most fruitful period of theatrical production between 1833 and 1834 — respond to their obstacles with sophisticated, 'theatricalized' strategies. The relationship between stage and world is explicitly questioned in these plays, where characters paradoxically try to access something 'authentic' through performance. Only Fantasio will succeed.

Sacrifice, as defined by Bataille, Girard and Scarry and as indeed is evidenced by its etymology, is about 'making sacred'. For Bataille, sacrifice is the act in which the community of discontinuous individuals gathers to watch death, to experience in common the vertigo of the abyss of death as one member, or a substitute, goes over the edge of the precipice into continuity. For Girard, sacrifice is an act in which the community gives up one of its members (or again, a substitute) in order to appease its own violence and to save itself from that violence. For Scarry, sacrifice is an act by which a body is physically opened so that its radical embodiment can be read as proof of some unembodied concept. All these theorists have in common the sense that sacrifice is a performance shared by a community and that its result is the production of meaning. The ability to agree upon meaning(s) is, in fact, the necessary condition for all community; it is the first product that makes the production and exchange of all other products possible.

The substitution of a victim representing either the community as a whole, in Bataille and Girard's models, or representing the claims of that community, in Scarry's model, is the religious analogue to the substitutions, which in three of Musset's plays, lead to the deaths of one of the doubled figures. Substitutions take place within the highly ritualised and over-determined field of theatre and lead not to proof of some unanchored claim, as in the plays discussed in Chapter One, but to the impossibility of further communication. All exchange between would-be lovers ends with the deaths of Cœlio and Rosette; their deaths fail to translate as sacrifices to the possibility of love among the survivors and instead the dead separate the living forever. In staging sacrifices in such self-consciously theatrical plays, Musset evokes the very origins of theatre in a characteristically nostalgic move towards a mythic past where the sacred was supposedly alive in the body of a divinely appointed king. Yet these modern sacrifices always fail; the sacred remains inaccessible and the past remains an insubstantial myth. In this chapter, then, we will explore the idea of performance and its relationship to the real, and we will analyze the death of the doubles in terms of sacrifice in order to determine the meaning of an inefficacious sacrifice for the individual, for the theatrical audience, and for the culture.

Part One. Ritual and Meaning: Les Caprices de Marianne

First published in *La Revue des Deux Mondes* in 1833, *Les Caprices de Marianne* definitively marks the beginning of Musset's mature period. In his earlier dramatic works in verse Musset fails to craft compelling plots, and in his early works in prose Musset's sometimes heavy-handed lyricism tends to interrupt the action of the play. Here, for the first time, Musset is able to adapt his language to the theatrical form without sacrificing either poetic refinement or dramatic force. This play in prose went through several versions during the life of the author, including an 1851 scenic version which reduced the number of sets to one and purged the play of some of the details which the censors had found unacceptable, particularly Octave's views on love. It was successfully produced that same year at the Comédie Française, at the time called the Théâtre de la République; however, both David Sices in his monograph on Musset[1] and Simon Jeune in his notes to the Pléiade edition of the play argue that the scenic version is inferior, lacking the audacity of the anterior versions due to the procrustean restraints of the contemporary stage. Regardless of the nineteenth-century distinction between dramatic texts destined for production and those meant only for reading — a distinction which Musset himself maintained throughout his career — it is the version of Musset's first mature comedy destined only for reading which is most often performed today and which has achieved the status of *theatrical* masterpiece.[2]

The play is the story of Cœlio, a young Neapolitan in love with Marianne, the wife of the jealous judge Claudio. Unable to express him-

---

[1] David Sices, *Theatre of Solitude: the drama of Alfred de Musset* (Hanover: University Press of New England, 1974). For a comparison of the two main versions of the play, see his second chapter.

[2] There are technically three versions destined for reading which vary only slightly: the 1833 version which appeared in *La Revue des Deux Mondes,* the 1834 version which appeared in *Un Spectacle dans un fauteuil,* and the 1840 version which appeared in the collection *Comédies et proverbes.* This last is the text to which we will refer, as it is the text presented by Simon Jeune in the 1990 Pléiade. Maurice Allem in the 1952 Pléiade prefers to give the final, corrected scenic version from the 1853 edition of *Comédies et proverbes.* For a discussion of the differences between the versions, see the notes to Jeune's Pléiade, 911–3.

self in her presence, Cœlio enlists the aid of his eloquent friend Octave to plead his suit with Marianne. She falls in love with Octave, and, believing him to be in love with her as well, invites him to come to her garden after dark. Though Octave's feelings for Marianne are ambiguous, his loyalty to his friend prevails and he sends Cœlio to the meeting in his place. Marianne warns Octave too late that her husband is lying in wait to kill her suitor, and Claudio kills Cœlio before Octave arrives. In the final scene at Cœlio's tomb, Octave, who had earlier indicated an attraction to Marianne, refuses her advances saying, 'Je ne vous aime pas, Marianne; c'était Cœlio qui vous aimait.'[3]

From the beginning, Cœlio's beliefs about love are coloured by ideas of sacrifice. In his Act One, scene ii conversation with Hermia, his mother, we see Cœlio already rehearsing the unfortunate outcome of his own romance as he asks her to tell the love story from her past, a story he has clearly heard before. 'Ô ma mère!' he exclaims, 'vous avez inspiré l'amour! ... vous n'avez point aimé; un parent de mon père est mort d'amour pour vous.'[4] Hermia then goes on to tell the story of her first romantic intrigue, which bears more than a coincidental resemblance to Cœlio's. Her suitor, Orsini, had engaged the young man who would later become Cœlio's father to woo on his behalf, but Hermia refused Orsini and married Cœlio's father instead. Orsini could not bear the rejection; later, 'on trouva dans sa chambre le pauvre jeune homme traversé de part en part de plusieurs coups d'épée.'[5] Cœlio clearly identifies with Orsini and believes his love for Marianne to be as impossible as Orsini's (and arguably his own) love for Hermia. The object of love, the mother or her substitute, is inaccessible because of the obstacle of the father, but the retelling of the story offers the hope that inaccessibility can be conjured by the magic of sacrifice. For though Orsini did not possess Hermia in life, his death translates into a transcendent and eternal bond between the young man and his love object. Throughout her telling of the story, Hermia repeats Orsini's name over and over, while referring to Cœlio's father only as 'votre père'. In asking to hear Hermia's story again, Cœlio is,

---

[3] Musset, *Théâtre complet* (Paris: Gallimard, 1990), 101.
[4] Ibid., 81.
[5] Ibid., 82.

on the one hand, steeling himself to his task (his imminent death) and on the other hand, reminding himself how it will all be worthwhile.

Cœlio's love is based on the idea of repetition, the modelling of his mother's experience, and the very possibility of love implies for him the necessity of sacrifice. Later in the play Cœlio exclaims:

> Ah que je fusse né dans le temps des tournois et des batailles! Qu'il m'eût été permis de porter les couleurs de Marianne et de les teindre de mon sang! Qu'on m'eût donné un rival à combattre, une armée entière à défier! Que le sacrifice de ma vie eût pu lui être utile! Je sais agir, mais je ne puis parler. Ma langue ne sert point mon cœur, et je mourrai sans m'être fait comprendre, comme un muet dans une prison.[6]

Cœlio laments that the courtly love code is no longer pertinent, that love is spoken and not expressed by bodily engagement: the wearing of colours, the spilling of blood, the sacrifice of a life. Once again we are reminded of Elaine Scarry's insistence on the body / voice dichotomy in the occidental imaginary. But whereas in Scarry the sacrifice of a body makes real what is abstract or 'all voice', here, Cœlio's love encounters the dual obstacles of his personal inarticulateness and the shifting culture's failure to provide a physical vocabulary through which the sacrifice of his body might be understood.

While Cœlio is thus preparing for the sacrifice to come, Marianne and Octave are preparing a different kind of ritual, their own initiation to love. Since Marianne only appears in public on her way to and from church, her conversations with Octave are measured according to ecclesiastical time, their first encounter taking place at the end of matins, their second and third as she goes to and from vespers. Their wooing is from the outset inscribed in a system of ritual, and in this way Marianne's seduction represents her initiation into the possibility of sensual pleasure. In sharp contrast to Marianne's nearly cloistered existence is Octave's dissolute lifestyle; he is drunk at his first entrance and brags to Cœlio that he has not been home in a week (Act I, scene i). Like Marianne, however, over the course of his conversations with her, Octave will learn about love.

[6] Ibid. 92

Significantly, their fourth meeting takes place not in the public space between Marianne's house and the church, but in the private space of Marianne's own drawing room. The seduction's operation is double and antagonistic, growing out of the witty sparring that characterises the potential lovers' meetings; in the end, Marianne will be lured out of her chosen path of prudery and Octave invited in to experience 'true love' beyond mere sensual pleasure.

Throughout the course of his seduction of Marianne, however, Octave reveals an understanding of love which stands in opposition to Cœlio's. In Act II, scene i, Marianne begins a comparison of wine and women which Octave extends into a paean on wine. He argues that different from women, wine needs no wooing, that the bottle knows 'qu'elle est bonne à boire et qu'elle est faite pour être bue'.[7] It is the fate of both, presumably, like the bottle in Octave's extended metaphor, to 'donner un quart d'heure d'oubli, et mourir',[8] but the wine does so more readily. Moreover, Octave's preferred wine is 'lacryma-christi',[9] evoking in its name the quintessential sacrificial victim. Yet the time limit set by Octave, 'un quart d'heure', shows the radical break between the two friends' ideas about sacrifice. Cœlio believes in a love that transcends the moment and through death conquers time. Octave believes only in the temporary drunkenness of physical pleasure, though he tries his best to extend that pleasure beyond all reasonable limits. However, while it is Cœlio who expresses concern about his friend's lifestyle, 'Huit jours hors de chez toi! Tu te tueras, Octave',[10] in the end, only Cœlio will succumb to his passion.

Marianne herself finally gives in and decides to take a lover, but it is not in response to Octave's / Cœlio's wooing as much as it is in response to her husband's intolerable jealousy. When she invites Octave into her drawing room and announces that she is ready to listen to Cœlio's declaration, Marianne is merely acting out a script. Since the role of 'dragon de

---

[7] Ibid., 91.
[8] Ibid.
[9] Ibid., 87.
[10] Ibid., 74.

vertu'[11] did not earn for her Claudio's respect, she will now try the role of adulteress. 'Tenez, voilà mon écharpe en gage',[12] she tells Octave, as if following the script of the courtly love tradition to which Cœlio also aspires. But the line between acting and real feeling is soon blurred. Octave, overcome by her change of heart, falls to his knees and speaks with more passion than ever about the love Cœlio bears her, evoking her situation with a sympathy that finally succeeds in moving her. 'Vous, si belle, si jeune, si pure encore, livrée à un vieillard qui n'a plus de sens et qui n'a jamais eu de cœur! Si vous saviez quel trésor de bonheur, quelle mine féconde repose en vous! en lui! dans cette fraîche aurore de jeunesse, dans cette rosée céleste de la vie, dans ce premier accord de deux âmes jumelles!'[13] Of course, as Cœlio had predicted from the beginning, the love Octave awakens is for himself and not for his friend. Marianne, understanding the delicate situation between the friends and sure that Octave shares the feeling he has just inspired, attempts to simplify matters for Octave: 'Cœlio me déplaît; je ne veux pas de lui. Parlez-moi de quelque autre, de qui vous voudrez. Choisissez-moi dans vos amis un cavalier digne de moi; envoyez-le-moi, Octave.'[14] While Octave does not hesitate to disregard Marianne's orders and send his friend to the meeting in his place, in his soliloquy in Act II, scene iv he expresses some regret. 'Comme tu m'aurais détesté, Marianne, si je t'avais aimée! comme tu m'aurais fermé ta porte! comme ton bélître de mari t'aurait paru un Adonis, un Sylvain, en comparaison de moi!'[15] It seems that, after all, Octave has developed an ability, if not to love Marianne, at least to appreciate her; for though he seems not to regret sending Cœlio to the tryst, he clearly regrets that he himself is unworthy to go.

So a first, complicated set of substitutions has already taken place. Octave has stood in for Cœlio in the seduction; Cœlio is to stand in for Octave in love. But with the intervention of the jealousy of Claudio, this final substitution will conclude in the sacrificial death of Cœlio. When

[11] Ibid., 73.
[12] Ibid., 95.
[13] Ibid.
[14] Ibid., 74.
[15] Ibid., 98.

Cœlio arrives beneath Marianne's window, she calls out Octave's name and exhorts him to flee. Here, the doubling which has characterised Octave and Cœlio's relationship reaches its most extreme conclusion as, in his response, Cœlio himself proves momentarily unable to distinguish between himself and his double: 'Seigneur mon Dieu? quel nom ai-je entendu? ... Est-ce un rêve? suis-je Cœlio?'[16] Faced with death, Cœlio suddenly understands, and in apostrophe to his friend, accuses him of having planned the ambush: 'Octave, traître Octave, puisse mon sang retomber sur toi! Puisque tu savais quel sort m'attendait ici, et que tu m'y as envoyé à ta place, tu seras satisfait dans ton désir.'[17] From Cœlio's point of view, Claudio's participation is irrelevant; Octave is the architect of his friend's death, and Claudio is but the means to that end. While this is not the case, it matters that Cœlio believes it to be so and that, though not without bitterness at his deception, he welcomes death. In this way, Cœlio's death corresponds directly to the suicide of Orsini which has been his explicit model from the beginning and to the structure of sacrifice, in which the assent of the victim is obligatory.

The substitution here is structured by doubling: the heroes substitute for one another, Octave taking Cœlio's place at the head of his table, Cœlio taking Octave's in Marianne's garden; there are two messages delivered simultaneously that a lover is expected: by Marianne in one case and by Claudio in the other. The ultimate removal of Cœlio should 'resolve the numbers', according to the model presented by Hermia's story, eliminating the now unnecessary doubled lover and leaving only a happy couple. Just as Octave doubles Cœlio in the present, the entire configuration Octave-Cœlio-Marianne doubles the configuration Cœlio's father-Orsini-Hermia in the past. In this way, though Cœlio is physically removed by death, the sacrificial nature of his death (dying for love and in lieu of his best friend) should paradoxically solidify his place in Marianne's heart, allowing him to possess her through the proved enormity of his love in the story that will be told between the lovers later. But this is not at all what comes to pass.

[16] Ibid., 99.
[17] Ibid.

For Scarry, as we have seen, there are two parts to sacrifice: the body which is opened up and the story told about it. The sacrifice in fact confers reality onto the story, proving its truth through its proximity to the opened body. Reciprocally, the story explains the sacrifice, conferring a kind of transcendence on the ritualised death. Referring to the Biblical story of Abraham and Isaac, she writes, 'It is in [the act of imagining] that Isaac yields against all phenomenal assessment to Abraham, that Abraham yields to God, and that the reader yields to the narrative.'[18] The role played in Scarry's example by the reader of the Bible is analogous to the role played by the witness to the sacrifice, who reads the sacrificed body and understands that it makes the story so. What happens in the last scene of *Les Caprices de Marianne* is that Octave (and perhaps the reader or the audience in the theatre) attempts but fails to create such a story about Cœlio's death, to confer meaning on the events of the play. This failure can be read either as the failure of the sacrifice itself, or as the failure of the survivors to derive meaning from the sacrifice.

In *La Violence et le sacré,* René Girard argues that the key characteristic of the sacrificial victim is that avenging him or her (or it) be impossible: 'la seule qu'on puisse frapper sans danger car il n'y aura personne pour épouser sa cause.'[19] This is important, for, according to Girard, sacrifice is meant precisely to prevent the unchaining of violence in an endless series of acts of retribution. 'C'est la communauté entière que le sacrifice protège de *sa* propre violence, c'est la communauté entière qu'il détourne vers des victimes qui lui sont extérieures. Le sacrifice polarise sur la victime des germes de dissension partout répandus et il les dissipe en leur proposant un assouvissement partiel.'[20] However, while Claudio's sacrifice of Cœlio 'works' on one level, as the violence indeed ends there, it fails to create or reactivate any kind of community, which in Scarry's terms would be 'meaning'. Indeed, it would be difficult to argue that the addle-brained Claudio had such a purpose in mind. This particular sacrifice lacks a performative dimension; without the community to witness

---

[18] Elaine Scarry, *The Body in Pain* (New York: Oxford University Press, 1985), 205.
[19] René Girard, *La Violence et le sacré* (Paris: Éditions du monde, 1972), 26–27.
[20] Ibid., 18.

the death of the victim, that death is without effect within the community. So although we have argued from the beginning that Cœlio's death is a sacrifice performed within the context of ritual, the lack of coherent participation by the community renders the death of Cœlio meaningless and unworthy of the category 'sacrifice'.[21]

A more complicated obstacle to the production of meaning lies in Octave's extreme, almost absurd, identification with the victim, which forces him to relinquish his position as survivor and therefore his abilities and responsibilities. 'Ce tombeau m'appartient: c'est moi qu'ils ont étendu sous cette froide pierre; c'est pour moi qu'ils avaient aiguisé leurs épées; c'est moi qu'ils ont tué',[22] laments Octave. Bataille argues in *L'Érotisme* that identification with the victim is an essential element of sacrifice because it is identification that allows the spectator (or the *sacrificateur*) access to the *expérience des limites* of the other; however Octave's identification with Cœlio surpasses this temporary empathy. According to Bataille, as noted earlier, the essential truth of human discontinuity is: 'Si vous mourez, ce n'est pas moi qui meurs,'[23] but Octave refuses this distinction. In claiming Cœlio's death as his own, Octave chooses to place himself beyond responsibility in a move that represents the most radical expression of his characteristic refusal to engage in life.

For while Cœlio has submitted his body to his belief in love and transcendence, Octave has only engaged his voice with Marianne. Moreover, though Octave's love for Cœlio is apparent throughout his eulogy, he refuses the engagement of his body on his friend's behalf. 'Cœlio m'aurait vengé si j'étais mort pour lui comme il est mort pour moi.'[24] Octave's position is paradoxical: he admires Cœlio's way of loving: 'J'aime ton amour, Cœlio: il divague dans ta cervelle comme un flacon syracusain',[25] but the act of loving or of dying for love (or friendship or any other prin-

---

[21] We might argue that the audience in the theatre could or should stand in for this 'community', and that having witnessed the sacrifice, it is up to them to establish 'meaning' for it.
[22] Musset, Théâtre, 101.
[23] Georges Bataille, *L'Érotisme* (Paris: Éditions de Minuit, 1957), 17.
[24] Musset, Théâtre, 101.
[25] Ibid., 76.

ciple) is beyond him. And what is required to make Cœlio's death meaningful is the continuation of the system by which bodies come to have meaning: the system of sacrifice. Octave would have to engage his body either to avenge his friend or to love Marianne, and he can do neither.

In his famous Act I, scene i metaphor of the tightrope walker, Octave describes himself as a performer involved in a dangerous game.

> Figure-toi un danseur de corde, en brodequins d'argent, le balancier au poing, suspendu entre le ciel et la terre; ... toute une légion de monstres se suspendent à son manteau et le tiraillent de tous côtés pour lui faire perdre l'équilibre; des phrases redondantes, de grands mots enchâssés cavalcadent autour de lui; une nuée de prédictions sinistres l'aveugle de ses ailes noires. Il continue sa course légère de l'orient à l'occident. S'il regarde en bas, la tête lui tourne; s'il regarde en haut, le pied lui manque. Il va plus vite que le vent, et toutes les mains tendues autour de lui ne lui feront pas renverser une goutte de la coupe joyeuse qu'il porte à la sienne. Voilà ma vie, mon cher ami; c'est ma fidèle image que tu vois.[26]

Octave as performer must stay above the fray, *not* experience love or communication. He must not believe in the 'phrases redondantes, de grands mots enchâssés [qui] cavalcadent autour de lui;' he must simply keep moving forward, keep performing. Cœlio, on the other hand, participates in the various systems (courtship, honour, sacrifice) despite the danger of falling; according to Octave's eulogy, '[Cœlio] savait combien les illusions sont trompeuses, et il préférait ses illusions à la réalité.'[27] But our terms, if not our tightrope walker, have slipped. Cœlio is supposed to be the one who loves concretely, whose body stands for the proof of the truth of his love, and yet Octave says that he engages in *illusion* which he prefers to reality. Does this mean that Cœlio's love for Marianne was not 'true'? No, Octave's statement is even more radical: he means that believing in love, engaging one's body as proof is an illusion, that there is no such thing as transcendent love and even sacrificial death cannot make it so. Octave wants to believe in real love (in Cœlio's love for Marianne which is the last word of the play) and yet cannot engage his own body to

---

[26] Ibid., 74.
[27] Ibid., 100.

continue the meaning-making process begun by Cœlio's death, to make that death into a coherent story he can share with Marianne. The point of performance (theatrical or ritual / sacrificial) is to concretise something abstract, to make it mean something (temporarily in the case of theatrical performance, transcendently in the case of the ritual / sacrifice). But Musset's play eschews meaning, stays somehow above the fray, like the tightrope walker, in the rarefied air where absurdity is the rule. Sacrifice becomes just another performance; it loses its unique, transcendent status and is relegated to the contingent and relative position of just another play, one not structured by sacrifice.

In a way, the lesson of *Les Caprices de Marianne* is that acting in the world is acting, and the sacred cannot be operative in an absurd world where life and stage are one. Performance allows the subject to create only a temporarily believable fiction. Hermia's story inspires the desire to love in Cœlio and Octave's speeches inspire love in Marianne: these performances provide the characters with access to a limited kind of meaning (Octave's 'quart d'heure d'oubli'), which is perhaps the only meaning possible. If sacrifice fails to provide the characters access to transcendent truth, playacting succeeds only too well in creating the temporary belief that makes their ultimate disillusion all the more devastating.

Part Two. Ritual and Performance: On ne badine pas avec l'amour

On ne badine pas avec l'amour first appeared in *La Revue des Deux Mondes* in 1834, with the generic marker of *proverbe*. However, classifying this play is problematic, for like *Les Caprices de Marianne*, it opens with a highly stylised comedic structure and then undermines it in a tragic dénouement. The play is the story of two young cousins, Perdican and Camille, destined by Perdican's father, the Baron, to wed one another. They arrive at the Baron's house separately after a long absence and rather than immediately accepting the Baron's wishes for their future, they begin a series of negotiations to determine their own future. In a plot that resembles the 'proof plots' we discussed in Chapter One, Camille tests Perdican's attachment by telling him she plans to enter the convent. Perdican, hurt by Camille's rejection, renews his friendship with Rosette, a peasant and Camille's *sœur de lait*. After he promises to marry Rosette,

Perdican finally confesses his love to Camille, but Rosette overhears and dies instantly of a broken heart. Her death separates the lovers irrevocably and the play closes on Camille's famous line: 'Elle est morte! Adieu, Perdican!'[28]

Though both plays conclude with the death of a double and both allude to sacrifice in the form that the death takes, the role of sacrifice differs in *Les Caprices de Marianne* and in *On ne badine pas avec l'amour*. In the former, Cœlio consciously chooses to make his death conform to a sacrificial structure; his death is foreshadowed in Hermia's story; he accepts death at the hand of Claudio, and he hopes all the while that his death will, like the death enacted in sacrifice, mean something. In *On ne badine pas avec l'amour,* sacrifice is not explicitly invoked. Perdican and Camille are both searching for some evidence that will substantiate the truth about love: Do we feel it? Is it real? Can it last? As they debate these questions, they manufacture scenes through which they hope to surprise the truth, but they have no idea that their *mise-en-scène* will lead to a real death. It is as if the sacred erupts into their game when they find Rosette dead behind the altar; suddenly, there is proof, but of what? Different from Cœlio's death, Rosette's death means something for the couple who, but for her death, would have been united; but the complicated relationship between performance and the real in this play makes its abrupt conclusion anything but obvious.

In Scarry's analysis of the structure of belief, the sacrifice is used to substantiate the abstract idea of God. The first step is analogical verification, as we discussed in Chapter One, by which the body of the victim is understood to stand in for the body of God. The second movement, the one that concerns us more here, is the obfuscation of the origin of sacrifice that follows from belief in it. That the idea of God is the product of human imagining is completely effaced in the performance of the sacrifice. The made object becomes the Maker, and the fiction of sacrifice becomes the sign of the real. We need to explore the question of performance and the real in *On ne badine pas avec l'amour* in order to understand exactly what Rosette's death proves and why, instead of ena-

---

[28] Ibid., 298.

bling the perfect Marivaudian ending (boy and girl of the same class wed), it is experienced as the ultimate obstacle to love. Throughout the play, Perdican and Camille are trying to find a way to act 'authentically', out of real feeling instead of out of duty. Paradoxically, however, they rely on artifice to do it, as both stage scenes in which they attempt to trick the other into manifesting his or her real feelings. Their obsession with performance is figured structurally into the play as a whole. The rigid symmetry of the opening scenes, the play of the puppet characters or *fantoches,* and the general *comedia dell'arte* mood all highlight the theatrical aspects of the play. The use of a chorus, too, as mediator between the concerns of the stage world and the concerns of the audience, evokes the ancient theatre, which we have argued in turn evokes the ritual function of theatre; though here it does so only obliquely. Still, at every level, this is a play that is posing questions about theatre and the power of performance.

Artifice is posed explicitly as the opposite term to nature in the contrast which develops between the doubled heroines, Camille and Rosette.[29] Rosette responds to Perdican with unrehearsed simplicity, accepting his affections but rejecting his sophistic arguments about fraternal attachment. 'Les mots sont les mots', she warns, 'et des baisers sont des baisers'.[30] Her candour cuts through Perdican's posturing and provides the only example of disinterestedness in the play. Meanwhile, Camille plots and strategises to the point where it is not clear to the audience (or to any of the doubles for the audience within the play) when she is telling the truth and when she is attempting to elicit a given reaction. It eventually becomes clear, however, that Camille's artfulness is the product of her own ambivalence faced with her choices in life: love or the convent. She

---

[29]   In his article 'Le Théâtre à l'essai', Loïc Chotard argues that the opposition between artifice and nature is the central conflict of the play, representing the choice the hero must make between Camille and Rosette. This otherwise rich and admirable article fails to address the question of Camille's subjectivity and the choice she, herself, is trying to make. Moreover, as I will argue, the logic of the play simply does not sustain the artifice / nature opposition. The article appears in *Musset*: Lorenzaccio, On ne badine pas avec l'amour, Michel Crouzet (éd.), (Paris: SEDES, 1990), 25–43.

[30]   Musset, *Théâtre*, 269.

plans her conversation with Perdican at the fountain carefully, choosing the exact location to produce the maximum effect by awakening childhood memories: 'Est-ce possible? Est-ce toi, Camille, que je vois dans cette fontaine, assise sur les marguerites, comme aux jours d'autrefois?'[31] Moreover, while the conversation proceeds from her request for Perdican's 'avis', about whether or not she should become a nun, it is clearly directed by Camille in such a way that Perdican cannot fail to second her choice of the convent. At the same time, however, her main reason for refusing Perdican's hand is ironically that *men* are deceitful in love.

Camille is looking for a love with an inalienable value and sets up an opposition between Christian love, which is transcendent because substantiated by sacrifice, and the love of men, which is temporary and without intrinsic value. She shows Perdican her crucifix and declares: 'Je veux aimer d'un amour éternel, et faire des serments qui ne se violent pas. Voilà mon amant,'[32] she declares. Following her own argument, Camille's only logical choice is to go back to the convent, to remove herself from what she considers to be a degrading and compromising circulation. 'Est-ce donc une monnaie que votre amour, pour qu'il puisse passer ainsi de mains en mains jusqu'à la mort?' she asks Perdican and then answers for herself, 'Non, ce n'est pas même une monnaie, car la plus mince pièce d'or vaut mieux que vous, et, dans quelques mains qu'elle passe, elle garde son effigie.'[33] But Perdican is able to shift the terms of the argument away from his own past and reveal the selfishness of the cloistered ladies who had shared their unfortunate love stories with the impressionable Camille in order to awaken bittersweet memories for themselves. 'Elles t'ont montré avec horreur la route de leur vie; tu t'es signée devant leurs cicatrices, comme devant les plaies de Jésus.'[34] These wounds of love are not proof of the perfidy of men; he seems to say, but somewhat pleasant reminders of a vanished happiness. So the system that Camille denounces — the artifice of *le monde* which she claims to have renounced — is reproduced within the convent walls and at the base of the

[31] Ibid., 273.
[32] Ibid., 277.
[33] Ibid., 278.
[34] Ibid., 279.

system there is no transcendence at all. 'Elles qui te représentent l'amour des hommes comme un mensonge, savent-elles qu'il y a pis encore, le mensonge de l'amour divin?'[35] There seems to be no outside of artifice.

To combat Camille's arguments in favour of retreat from the world, Perdican offers the idea of active engagement. Perdican argues passionately that love is what allows one to say, in the end: 'J'ai souffert souvent, je me suis trompé quelquefois, mais j'ai aimé. C'est moi qui ai vécu, et non pas un être factice créé par mon orgueil et mon ennui.'[36] We have to act, says Perdican, to fool and be fooled or we are living only a shadow life; we are not our 'real' selves. He skilfully recalibrates the terms of the argument such that the false life, that led by an 'être factice' is the life that avoids acting and loving in the world. That this acting might also involve artifice is of secondary concern because a greater truth is achieved through the experiences of the lovers. The wounds of love, then, are not stigmata, a woman's punishment for believing in the lies of men, but proof of life itself. For Perdican, regardless of the consequences, the game of love is not placed in opposition to the 'natural' but as a necessary component of the 'natural' system. [37]

In this discussion Perdican and Camille touch only indirectly on the idea of sacrifice as it relates to the question of authenticity and performance. If only we could prove that love (even temporary love) exists, Perdican seems to say, we could be sure that our lives are real and meaningful. In his 'Lascaux, ou la naissance de l'art', Georges Bataille

---

[35] Ibid., 280.
[36] Ibid.
[37] Musset reproduces here lines from a letter written him by George Sand (12 May 1834), after the rupture in Venice, but before the definitive end of their liaison in 1835. See Simon Jeune's notes to the Pléiade edition, pages 1065–6 and the *chronologie* in the same volume, p. XLI. The quotation serves a complicated proof function within the play, for while on the one hand Musset seems to be arguing in favour of a certain kind of artifice as necessary to the creation of the 'real' feelings of love, the quotation from his real relationship with George Sand erupts into the fictional world as 'proof' of the author's experience and therefore proof somehow of the truth enacted in the play. That the consequences of the Musset / Sand relationship and rupture were severe in the lives (and careers) of the two and that the consequences of the brief Perdican / Camille relationship are even more severe is no coincidence.

proposes a way of looking at artifice such that it need not be the negative term in a dichotomy with nature. He argues that art (or artifice or play of any kind)[38] does not arise in opposition to nature, but to utilitarian activity. '[L'art] a, par rapport à l'activité utilitaire, la valeur d'une opposition: c'est une protestation contre un monde qui existait, mais sans lequel la protestation elle-même n'aurait pu prendre corps.'[39] For Bataille, art and play, conceived in their ritual function, give access from the world of the profane into the world of the sacred, that realm where a community enacts meaning. In this way, the object of art is 'la création d'une réalité sensible, modifiant le monde dans le sens d'une réponse au désir de prodige, impliqué dans l'essence de l'être humain.'[40]

In a way, this is what Perdican and Camille are trying to do. Through play, they are trying to get beyond utilitarian activity (the duty to marry imposed by the Baron) to a real, effusive love. Camille wavers, not sure if real love lies with Perdican or with God; Perdican wavers, not sure if real love lies with Camille or Rosette. Finally, it is when the two stop performing that their feelings become clear. The play's final scene opens with Camille in prayer. Her ambivalence is still unresolved, the role she has adopted having only succeeded in confusing her utterly. She cries out to God: 'Oh! pourquoi faites-vous mentir la vérité elle-même?'[41] She is unaware that she has an audience but Perdican overhears, understands and confesses his love. However, the two are unaware that they have an audience; Rosette overhears, understands and cries out from behind the altar. For all of their confusion and ambivalence up to this point, Camille and Perdican both understand immediately that Rosette's death will mean their eternal separation. 'Il me semble que mes mains sont couvertes de sang,'[42] says Perdican, before he is certain of Rosette's fate. As Camille

---

[38] Bataille does not distinguish between art and play, but instead argues: 'Ce que l'art est tout d'abord, et ce qu'il demeure avant tout, est un jeu', in Georges Bataille, *Œuvres complètes* (Paris: Gallimard, 1979), IX, 28.
[39] Ibid.
[40] Ibid., 37.
[41] Musset, *Théâtre*, 296.
[42] Ibid., 297.

exits to check on her, Perdican offers his own prayer and begs, 'Ne faites pas de moi un meurtrier!'⁴³

Bataille offers a possibility of considering this death as a sacrifice still, because, as he notes, the movement into the sacred cannot occur without transgression. 'L'antiquité voyait dans le sacrifice le *crime* du sacrificateur qui, dans le silence angoissé des assistants, mettait la victime à mort, le crime où le sacrificateur, en connaissance de cause et lui-même angoissé, violait l'interdit du meurtre. Il nous importe ici que, dans son essence, et dans la pratique, l'art exprime ce moment de transgression religieuse'.⁴⁴ From the very beginning, everything in the play — the children's education, the Baron's careful preparations, the lovers' scheming — has all been preparing for this real moment when, at the altar, Camille and Perdican would speak words of love so meaningful, so true that their union would be sanctified. The chorus tells us from the beginning that the play is to take place under the sign of festival: 'Ou je me trompe fort, ou quelque joyeuse bombance est dans l'air d'aujourd'hui.'⁴⁵ So the death of Rosette in a chapel, behind the altar, could be explained as a kind of expenditure, required by the community in obedience to 'l'exigence d'un monde plus profond, plus riche et prodigieux, l'exigence, en un mot, d'un monde sacré.'⁴⁶

It seems to me, however, that if we want to read Rosette's death as a sacrifice, we would need to locate a sanctifying effect of her death on Camille and Perdican's love, and as we have seen, it has rather the opposite effect. What Bataille argues is that sacrifice does not cease to be a crime under sacrificial conditions, but that the interdiction of murder (which is a necessary component of the sacrifice) is overcome by the community. Scarry explains this phenomenon as the process by which sacrifice succeeds in obscuring its own human origins to go beyond crime and cruelty and into the realm of meaning and transcendence. This is what she calls the work of belief or imagining. The games of Perdican and Camille, 'deux enfants insensés, et [qui ont] joué avec la vie et la

---

⁴³ Ibid., 298.
⁴⁴ Bataille (1979), 40–41.
⁴⁵ Musset, *Théâtre*, 255.
⁴⁶ Bataille (1979), 41.

mort',[47] are motivated by selfishness, jealousy and immaturity and simply fail to qualify as sacrifice. What we have here is not a sacrifice at all because its source is laid bare — whence the play's emphasis on theatrical structure and on artifice — lest it be mistaken that Rosette's death (even on an altar) is an act that sanctifies. Lest the victim be called willing and love transcendent.

The play's opening scenes lead us to expect a light-hearted little romp. So there is dissonance between our expectations and the seriousness of the consequences suffered by Camille, Perdican and especially Rosette, a dissonance which underscores the absurdity of this world where everything is staged as if to arrive at proof or meaning but out of which only chaos results. As in *Les Caprices de Marianne*, one is left disappointed, as if the world has shrunk to the dimensions of the stage, leaving only a series of actions and effects joined by theatrical convention. The seeming inability of these plays to transcend themselves or of the characters to go beyond the surface of their experience is simply absurd, almost maddening. It is the expression of Musset's deepest cynicism, which goes far beyond typical 'romantic ennui'. In these plays and to an even greater degree in *Lorenzaccio*, the playwright seems to say that love is possible, but powerless, that ritual is empty and that meaning is absent.

Part Three. Ritual and Self: Lorenzaccio

Musset's 1834 historical drama *Lorenzaccio* is generally considered to be the finest example of French Romantic theatre. The play, Musset's longest, recounts the last, desperate days of Lorenzo de Medicis who in 1537 assassinated his cousin, Alexandre de Medicis, duke of Florence. *Lorenzaccio* has long been characterised as the story of a young man's struggles with his society, with good and evil and with his own sense of self. Critics have themselves struggled to situate the meaning of virtue within the play and to explain Lorenzo's complicated motivation for committing a political murder that he himself predicts will have no political issue.[48]

---

[47] Musset, *Théâtre*, 298.
[48] Jeanne Bem's article '*Lorenzaccio*: entre l'histoire et le fantasme', *Poétique*, 11:

Lorenzo's descent from pure youth to debauched and turbulent courtier is mirrored in the perceived decline of Florence from republican virtue into tyrannical vice, which is also reflected in a generalised fall from grace of meaning, as sacred and immutable truth fragments into a multiplicity of competing and empty discourses. What is read as the decadence functioning at all levels of the play rests on a kind of nostalgia about the origins of the subject, of legitimate government and of sacred institutions which the play's conclusion reveals to have been unanchored myths. For Lorenzo, the murder of the duke, conceived as a sacrifice, represents the possibility of communicating with an original, unified self and of creating a coherent personal and political narrative. We will focus our reading on the questions of ideology and narrative in the search for self, a search that takes Lorenzo into the world of sacrifice, but fails to give him access to the sacred.

The play's five acts are divided into a total of thirty-eight densely populated scenes, and it seems that everyone in Florence is in one way or another plotting against the duke. Installed by Charles V and Pope Clement VII, Alexandre de Medicis, duke of Florence, is a debauched and cynical tyrant. While the Cardinal de Cibo manoeuvres to satisfy his own personal ambition in exerting power over the duke, other more Republican conspirators are plotting to usurp him entirely. Philippe Strozzi, patriarch of a large family and symbol of the virtuous old order of the Florentine republic, is tempted (by the death of his daughter at the hands of one of the duke's partisans) to raise an army among the ever-increasing number of banished; however, he hesitates and fails to act. Meanwhile, the Marquise de Cibo, sister-in-law of the cardinal, attempts to use her influence as the duke's mistress to persuade him to rule more wisely. It is finally the duke's cousin, Lorenzo, who commits the murder in a ritualised scene that has been characterised by critics as a sacrificial slaughter and as a darkly parodic wedding ceremony.[49] Political revolution does not

44 (November 1980), 451–61, is perhaps the richest and most innovative of recent years, though scholarship on *Lorenzaccio* is abundant.

[49] See, for example, Marie MacLean, 'The Sword and the Flower: the sexual symbolism of *Lorenzaccio*', *Australian Journal of French Studies*, 16: 2 (1979), 166–81, and Thérèse Malachy, 'Du Meurtre politique au sacrifice rituel', *Revue*

follow the assassination, however. Lorenzo flees to Venice where he is ignominiously thrown into the lagoon by a bounty-seeking mob, and the play closes on the elevation of the new duke, Côme de Medicis.

We mentioned briefly in our discussion of carnival in Hugo's works in Chapter Two that Musset was fascinated with carnival and specifically with Italy as the land of carnival and of sexual license. Here again, the play's Italian Renaissance setting evokes the festive, almost dreamlike quality associated with carnival. At the same time, however, the play recalls a darker Italian myth, of the warring Renaissance city-states, where conspiracies, poison and political rhetoric take centre stage.[50] In *Lorenzaccio* these two elements of the Italian mythos combine, creating a chiaroscuro effect against which the character of Lorenzo will suddenly, briefly become clear, only to dissolve back into the shadows. Innocent carnivalesque diversion or Machiavellian weapon, the mask, which appears in so many of Musset's other Italian plays, is here omnipresent. Lorenzo's main role, in which he pretends to be the duke's loyal friend in order to gain access to him and to assassinate him, spawns others. 'Pour plaire à mon cousin, il fallait arriver à lui, porté par les larmes des familles; pour devenir son ami, et acquérir sa confiance, il fallait baiser sur ses lèvres épaisses tous les restes de ses orgies,'[51] explains Lorenzo. To inspire the duke's gratitude, he plays the role of protector, denouncing various Republican conspirators, but in order to do that, he must play at winning the trust of the Republicans. Moreover, to win the duke's trust, he acts as his procurer and partner in debauchery, but to do this with impunity, he must inspire fear. 'Les lits des filles sont encore chauds de ma sueur, et les pères ne prennent pas, quand je passe, leurs couteaux et leurs balais pour m'assommer?',[52] he marvels to Philippe. Finally to make sure that no one suspects him of being capable of anything as diabolical and dangerous as his real project, Lorenzo feigns for everyone an exaggerated effeminacy, even fainting at the sight of a naked blade in Act I, scene v.

[50] *d'Histoire du théâtre*, 40: 3 (1988), 273–80.
This is also the setting for Hugo's 1833 historical drama, *Lucrèce Borgia*, one of Hugo's most successful productions.
[51] Musset, *Théâtre*, 200.
[52] Ibid., 201.

Lorenzo is not alone in wanting to rid Florence of the duke, who is considered 'un butor que le ciel avait fait pour être garçon boucher'[53] by the Orfèvre. In fact, each of the characters who aligns in opposition to the duke exhibits a nostalgic longing for the days before he took power. Philippe in particular blames Alexandre for the slip from virtue into vice that he perceives among the bourgeoisie. 'Ce qu'on appelle la vertu, est-ce donc l'habit du dimanche qu'on met pour aller à la messe?',[54] he ponders. And yet his opposition remains entirely discursive, as do, in some ways, his goals: 'La république, il nous faut ce mot-là.'[55] The Marquise, whose revolutionary activity is limited to lecturing the lascivious duke, also believes in the power of words: 'Ceux qui mettent les mots sur leur enclume, et qui les tordent avec un marteau et une lime, ne réfléchissent pas toujours que ces mots représentent des pensées, et ces pensées des actions.'[56]. She disapproves of the duke's behaviour, including his crossdressing and drunkenness, finding that 'nous sommes dans un triste temps pour toutes les choses saintes!'.[57] Decidedly, something is rotten in Florence, as it was in Denmark and in Thebes; and all of Florence hopes to restore the city by removing its morally infected leader.

Different from the deaths of Cœlio and of Rosette, the slaying of Alexandre is intended from the outset as a sacrifice by Lorenzo, and Philippe immediately sees in Alexandre's death the possibility of the expiation of the collective crimes of the city. The ritual elements of the murder of Alexandre have been discussed by many critics, so that we need only enumerate them here. First, the victim is specially chosen, as we have just mentioned, to play the scapegoat, to stand in for the crimes of all. The room is especially prepared, the lighting and flowers carefully chosen. Next, the victim is readied: having 'soupé comme trois moines',[58] he is presumably fatted; his sword is tied up and he is made to lie on his back, helpless. Finally he is put to death. Again, in all of Lorenzo's preparations

[53] Ibid., 144.
[54] Ibid., 163.
[55] Ibid., 164.
[56] Ibid., 149.
[57] Ibid.
[58] Ibid., 235.

we see the conflation of stage and altar, as the action is both scripted and carefully rehearsed. Roman history provides the script, and Brutus is Lorenzo's explicit role model, as we see in Act II, scene iv where Lorenzo discusses the story of Tarquin the Proud (recounted in Livy) with his mother and Catherine. The story is that of a debauched tyrant, one of the two figures of Roman history to be assassinated by a Brutus.[59] In Act III, scene iii, we learn that Lorenzo considers his role to be that of 'Brutus moderne',[60] and wonders only how Brutus, who feigned madness to beguile Tarquin, 'n'y ait pas laissé sa raison'.[61] In Act III, scene i, we see the Lorenzo who supposedly faints in the presence of a sword rehearsing his role of sacrificer, fencing ferociously with his valet Scoronconcolo. In the soliloquy preceding the murder Lorenzo obsesses like any director on opening night about the details of the production. Moreover the duke's question at the moment of the murder — 'C'est toi, Renzo?' recalls Julius Caesar's famous '*Et tu Brute?*' and in this way plays into the script that Lorenzo is attempting to live out.

When the sacrifice of the duke fails to bring about moral or political revolution in Florence, Philippe faults Lorenzo ironically for his *lack* of dramatic flair. 'Pourquoi n'es-tu pas sorti la tête du duc à la main? Le peuple t'aurait suivi comme son sauveur et son chef.'[62] At the same time, however, Lorenzo's performance leading up to the murder has made it impossible for him to be convincing in the role of liberator. When he attempts to alert the citizens to give them time to prepare the revolution, they do not take him seriously. 'C'est toi, Renzinaccio? ... Tu veux tuer le duc, toi? Allons donc!'[63] Lorenzo has played his role too well, and the truth is somehow lost in his playacting. Walter Moser characterises Lorenzo's Florence as 'le lieu où la vérité n'a pas sa place, où le sacré, comme garant suprême de tous les discours, aura tourné en mensonge et

---

[59] Roman history's implicit association with 'the sacred' here represents a movement back into the past (and from a viewpoint external to the play, this is the second such movement) in what we will see is a fruitless search for the origin (of subjectivity, of theatre, of action).
[60] Musset, *Théâtre*, 202.
[61] Ibid., 203.
[62] Ibid., 242.
[63] Ibid.. 228–9.

en mascarade'.⁶⁴ The performance of the sacrifice, which is supposed to substantiate the reality of virtue and the claims to virtue of the sacrificer, is, like the locked room in which Lorenzo leaves the body, without issue. If the sacrifice of the duke is ultimately a failure, it does at least manage to restore Lorenzo to himself and to his former beliefs about virtue and the world for one brief moment. Having killed the duke, Lorenzo goes to the window and exclaims, 'Que la nuit est belle! Que l'air du ciel est pur!'⁶⁵ Again this exemplifies the process Elaine Scarry calls analogical verification. Lorenzo reads the elimination of the duke, who was supposed to represent moral decay, in the purified air of the outside world, and, for one unsustainable moment, the sacrifice is meaningful. 'Quel moment!'⁶⁶ he cries, recalling the single moment of coherence enjoyed by the heroes in the plays we discussed in the first two chapters. In fact, the meaning that Lorenzo and Philippe would like the people to read into the death of the duke will be superseded by the machinations of the Cardinal de Cibo. The Cardinal takes control of the spectacle, hiding the duke's body from the populace until there is another duke already in place. The play closes on the ritualised elevation of that duke, a spectacle whose efficacy seems to second Philippe's criticism (that Lorenzo should have displayed the duke's body). At the same time, however, its empty formality reveals that the supposedly sacred ceremonies of Florence are merely in the service of the existing power structure, without any connection to transcendent values about government or virtue.

The failure of the sacrifice to bring about sustainable change is central to the play (even structurally as it is the subject of Act III, scene iii) because it is central to Lorenzo's role-playing and failed attempts at self-definition. Lorenzo does not expect that the murder of the duke will free Florence — he admits this to Philippe — but it is supposed to resolve the secret of his many roles. When Philippe asks him why he would commit a murder that he believes will be 'inutile à ta patrie',⁶⁷ Lorenzo indignantly

---

⁶⁴   Walter Moser, 'Le Carnaval et le Cardinal', *Romantisme*, 19 (1978), 96.
⁶⁵   Musset, *Théâtre*, 236.
⁶⁶   Ibid., 236.
⁶⁷   Ibid., 204.

replies, 'Veux-tu que je laisse mourir en silence l'énigme de ma vie?'[68] Lorenzo sees the lesson that the duke's murder will teach as, if not transparent, at least translatable into a narrative about his life. 'Que les hommes me comprennent ou non, qu'ils agissent ou n'agissent pas, j'aurai dit tout ce que j'ai à dire; je leur ferai tailler leurs plumes, si je ne leur fais pas nettoyer leurs piques.'[69]

Even in this confessional scene, however, Lorenzo's story of his pure childhood and of his rapid descent into vice does not present a coherent narrative of what Lorenzo was, what he hoped to become and what he now is. Rather his account of the epiphany that set him on his present course is problematic and further emphasises the underlying difficulty of self-definition through narrative. 'Assis dans les ruines du Colisée antique, je ne sais pourquoi je me levai; ... et je jurai qu'un des tyrans de ma patrie mourrait de ma main',[70] he proclaims. Lorenzo's transformation is, however, linked to nothing more than a vague idea about tyranny, inspired by the history of antiquity and figured in the picturesque setting of the ruined Coliseum. The relationship between antiquity and ritual is here revealed to be little more than cosmetic. If Lorenzo has pledged to kill 'un des tyrans', it matters little to him which one. 'J'ai voulu d'abord tuer Clément VII', he explains. 'Je n'ai pu le faire, parce qu'on m'a banni de Rome avant le temps.'[71] From its conception, then, Lorenzo's noble plan was never about freeing Florence but about defining himself as a tyrant-killer, as a Brutus, and therefore as *not* Lorenzo.

Indeed, from the moment the plan is hatched, Lorenzo experiences a transmutation. But this transmutation is also an alienation from himself:

> Tu ne saurais jamais, à moins d'être fou, de quelle nature est la pensée qui m'a travaillé. Pour comprendre l'exaltation fiévreuse qui a enfanté en moi le Lorenzo qui te parle, il faudrait que mon cerveau et mes entrailles fussent à nu sous un scalpel. Une statue qui descendrait de son piédestal pour marcher parmi les hommes sur la place publique, serait peut-être semblable à ce que

[68] Ibid., 205.
[69] Ibid.
[70] Ibid., 199.
[71] Ibid.

j'ai été, le jour où j'ai commencé à vivre avec cette idée: il faut que je sois un Brutus.⁷²

Clearly, Lorenzo feels divided against himself; there is one Lorenzo 'qui te parle' and another, older Lorenzo, who has experienced a sort of spiritual transformation. He feels not only different from what he used to be, but displaced and inhuman, like a statue off its pedestal.⁷³ The comparison to a statue works first generally as a comparison between the 'new' Lorenzo and a made art object, the product of his folly, second specifically as an allusion to the model he has chosen and which he makes explicit in the following line: Brutus. Not only is Lorenzo doubled, subject to a force outside himself, but his model is itself already doubled, as there are two Roman assassins named Brutus.

Bernard Masson has noted the importance of the proper name in Lorenzo's search for self. His alienation from that name is figured in the numerous nicknames and epithets corresponding to his many roles which he is given throughout the play.⁷⁴ To the duke, he is 'Renzo' or 'mignon;' to the courtiers, he is 'Lorenzetta' or 'l'homme sans épée;' and to the average citizens, he is the fearful 'Lorenzaccio'. Lorenzo's assassination of the duke is supposed to restore his 'good name' and win the esteem of the people of Florence. 'Il faut que le monde sache un peu qui je suis', he declares.⁷⁵ His victory is fleeting and hollow, however, for as Masson points out, his name is finally restored only in the death sentence read in Act V, scene ii. Elsewhere Masson argues that Lorenzo has lost the essential unity of self and that 'Par ce tyrannicide Lorenzo compte donner une unité formelle aux débris épars de sa personnalité et se proposer à lui-même le témoignage d'un accomplissement'.⁷⁶ His search for identity is a search for unity, is the search for the sacred. It is the ritualised, rehearsed

---

⁷² Ibid.
⁷³ See Anne Ubersfeld, 'Le Moi-statue', in *Journées d'études sur Alfred de Musset* (Clermont-Ferrand: Société des Études Romantiques, 1978), 63–79.
⁷⁴ Bernard Masson, *Musset et son double: Lecture de* Lorenzaccio (Paris: Librairie Minard, 1978).
⁷⁵ Musset, *Théâtre*, 205.
⁷⁶ Bernard Masson, 'Le Masque, le double et la personne dans quelques *Comédies et proverbes'*, *Revue des sciences humaines* (octobre-décembre 1962), 566.

performance of sacrifice that is to make possible a narrative that may be told about him afterwards and that Lorenzo hopes will structure his life and provide the 'unité formelle' which he lacks.

As we discussed in the first part of this chapter, Scarry's description of sacrifice has an important narrative component. The opening of the body of the victim is meant to substantiate or prove the story the witnesses / survivors need to tell about themselves, their community, their values or their God. In yielding to that narrative, the reader or audience participates in the sacrifice by allowing her body to be the site of belief in the sacrifice: 'the reader in his or her many capacities ceases to be the many things that he or she is and becomes in the stunned and exhausted silence of Genesis 22:1–19 the created offspring of the text'.[77] The theoretical pendant to Scarry's reading of sacrifice is her reading of Marx, which also relies on a certain understanding of narrative. Of *Das Kapital* she writes, 'If the monumentally complex substance of *Capital* were to be described in a single sentence, it could be described as an exhausting analysis of the steps and stages by which the obligatory referentiality of fictions ceases to be obligatory: it is an elaborate retracing of the path along which the reciprocity of artifice has lost its way back to its human source'.[78] By this she refers to the path of labour under capitalism, in which a person produces an object (which is a projection of the human body), which object becomes a commodity, sold for money, which money is then converted into capital and used to produce more money. Finally, the original object ceases to refer to the person whose labour originated it.[79] The process by which Lorenzo attempts to project himself onto the world, to create his identity as a commodity, exchangeable in the form of narrative ('je leur ferai tailler leurs plumes') is analogous to the path of labour under capitalism as charted by Marx. The artifice of the narratives Lorenzo and others invent (in his various roles, his confession, others' gossip and their insults) is underscored by the constantly circulating names and disguises which all purport to describe him as he *really* is. In attempting to (re)produce himself as a commodity, Lorenzo loses control

---

[77] Scarry (1985), 205.
[78] Ibid., 258.
[79] Ibid., 259.

of his narrative and it ceases to refer to him; instead it refers only to an empty ideology about tyrannicide and virtue which cannot be proved. Finally the murder of the duke takes Lorenzo into the ritualised world of sacrifice, which is supposed to guarantee the truth of exactly one story about Lorenzo. Instead, it proves only that Lorenzo's multiple names are equally without referents, that both the story of Lorenzo and the idea of Lorenzo are groundless. The ambiguity of Lorenzo's political motives as well as his attempt to *become* Brutus show to what degree he is already separated from himself and inhabited by the external forces of ideology, in Marx's sense. If that projected, made self still referred to the person pronouncing the words and performing the acts, there would be nothing amiss, but Lorenzo is without moorings. He refers to the murder as 'le seul fil qui rattache aujourd'hui mon cœur à quelques fibres de mon cœur d'autrefois',[80] and indeed once the murder is performed he is directionless. He tells Philippe, 'J'étais une machine à meurtre, mais à un meurtre seulement.'[81] With the death of Marie immediately following the murder, Lorenzo is utterly orphaned. He can no longer trace his path back to his origins, and although he may have re-conquered his name, it will not appear on a tombstone.

Lorenzo shows himself throughout the play to be obsessed with his own lack of substance and in fact his whole assassination plan can be read as a project whose object is to reaffirm his corporeality as identity. We first begin to understand the depth of Lorenzo's doubts about his body in his long confessional scene with Philippe, but they are indicated much earlier. In each of his appearances in the first three acts, Lorenzo's body is the site of his various disguises and commentaries on his disguises and is therefore a site of rather over-determined instability. Certainly, the duke sees him as insubstantial, referring to him first as 'l'ombre d'un ruffian' and then as a 'lendemain d'orgie ambulant'.[82] The other inhabitants of Florence, too, consider him to be of uncertain gender, a 'femmelette', which is later brought into sharp contrast with the exaggerated masculinity of the fencing scene with Scoronconcolo that opens Act III. All of

[80] Musset, *Théâtre*, 204.
[81] Ibid., 250.
[82] Ibid., 152.

these discourses about who Lorenzo is centre on his body as an indeterminate site; and later, his own discourse on vice centres on the body (both individual and politic) as the site of corruption and potentially of redemption.[83]

In Act II, Marie claims to have seen Lorenzo's spectre, her 'Lorenzino d'autrefois',[84] the image of him as he was before he began stalking the duke. Lorenzo's reaction is not the sceptical raillery we have already learned to expect from him, but a serious inquiry into what she saw. He even asks his mother to deliver a message to his phantom: 'Dites-lui qu'il verra bientôt quelque chose qui l'étonnera.'[85] Presumably, Lorenzo is cut off from this other self and it is only through Marie that he can hope to communicate with what he used to be. Later, in Act III, scene iii, Lorenzo claims that his *present* form is 'l'ombre de moi-même' and that what he hopes to revive in his murder of the duke is that other, more authentic self. 'Tu me demandes pourquoi je tue Alexandre? ... Veux-tu donc que je sois un spectre, et qu'en frappant sur ce squelette... il n'en sorte aucun son?'[86] Even Lorenzo seems not to know which is the body and which the shadow, but the duke's sacrificed body is supposed then somehow to restore Lorenzo's body to him. In all of his preparations for the murder Lorenzo identifies with his victim, imagining his reactions, predicting and diffusing his diffidence, and finally, locked in a struggle at the moment of the murder, shedding his own blood. 'Regarde, il m'a mordu au doigt. Je garderai jusqu'à la mort cette bague sanglante, inestimable diamant.'[87] His identification with the victim reaches its apex here as he conflates the duke's death with his own, but it was already present in his identification with the debauched lifestyle of Alexandre. In destroying Alexandre, his evil double on whom he has laid all of the blame for his own alienation, Lorenzo hopes to free himself of those other selves — the personae of his

---

[83] See Susan McCready, 'Power and Sexual Congress in Alfred de Musset's *Lorenzaccio*', *Romance Notes*, 44: 1 (Fall 2003), 83–91.
[84] Musset, *Théâtre*, 175.
[85] Ibid., 176.
[86] Ibid., 204.
[87] Ibid., 235.

many disguises and the corrupt courtier he has become — to become the one virtuous and solid Lorenzo his mother remembers.

We know the murder fails to resolve the many Lorenzos to one, integrated individual just as the sacrificial deaths of Cœlio and Rosette fail to reduce their respective cast of characters to one happy and united couple. Lorenzo's relationship to his mother (not unlike Cœlio's) is somehow the site of his hopes and ultimate failure at self-unification, as it is she alone who can see and communicate with the pure spectre from Lorenzo's past who represents the lost dream of unity. Significantly, Lorenzo fears for his mother's life before his murder of the duke: 'Que ma mère mourût de tout cela, voilà ce qui pourrait arriver.'[88] When he learns of the death of his mother, Lorenzo realises that his chance to communicate with the unified Lorenzo is lost forever: 'Je suis plus creux et plus vide qu'une statue de fer-blanc.'[89]

While Lorenzo is revealed to be constituted by the alienating ideologies of his culture he had attempted to exorcise, it may be argued that *Lorenzaccio* is similarly inhabited by the spectre of Shakespeare's *Hamlet*. It is Hamlet's task to exorcise that spectre, to put his father's spirit to rest by eliminating Claudius, the bad father, and in so doing to affirm his own self and claim his rights to succession, usurped by his uncle. The comparison between *Lorenzaccio* and *Hamlet* is not new, of course, and in fact it most often rests on a comparison of the two brooding, adolescent heroes. Both are thinkers, both mother-fixated, both planning a coup, both playing a variety of roles to do it. Yet these similarities do not support the conclusions of Cecil Malthus who writes,

> Shakespeare et Musset se font la même conception de l'homme... l'homme est une sorte de machine nerveuse, gouvernée par son tempérament, et emportée par ses passions sans frein. C'est un mélange de l'animal et du poète, dont le cerveau exalté s'emplit de visions douloureuses ou criminelles'.[90]

---

[88] Ibid., 231.
[89] Ibid., 250.
[90] Cecil Malthus, *Musset et Shakespeare: étude analytique de l'influence de Shakespeare sur le théâtre d'Alfred de Musset* (New York: Peter Lang, c. 1988), 115. This text was actually written during the 1930s and was published only posthumously.

Malthus is far from the only critic to make such sweeping claims, and like the usual definition of the 'romantic hero', his argument is based on a Cartesian notion of subjectivity. I want to argue for a redefinition of the romantic hero (which is perhaps the spectre haunting this project) in light of our contemporary understanding of subjectivity. We must go beyond the tautological identification of Lorenzo as romantic hero and begin to understand his subjectivity as a process rather than as a category.

At the level of our conception of subjectivity lie the most important differences between Hamlet and Lorenzo. We have argued that Lorenzo is in search of solidity, of a way to integrate the various stories about himself into a coherent narrative. Hamlet, on the other hand, laments, 'O, that this too too sullied flesh would melt, / Thaw and resolve itself into a dew' (Act I, scene ii).[91] At least until his father appears to give him a mission, he seeks dissolution in death, the end of all narrative. Second, and more relevant to us here is that the haunting of Hamlet by his father is qualitatively different from the hauntings in Florence. Naomi Schor argues that 'l'absence du père dans *Lorenzaccio* n'est qu'illusoire, superficielle',[92] because of the multiple occurrences of the word *père* in the text (far more than of *mère*), and because of the many father figures who surround Lorenzo. Certainly Schor's point is apt, and yet there is an essential difference between Hamlet's relationship to his ghostly father and Lorenzo's relationship to his multiple paternal models. The mute play that Hamlet directs in Act III, with which he hopes to 'catch the conscience of the king' is also explicitly meant as a way to test the veracity of the ghost's claims. Through the performance of the play and the reactions it elicits in Claudio, Hamlet can verify that the ghost is speaking transcendent truths and that the vengeance he enjoins Hamlet to commit is divine, not demonic. Lorenzo, on the other hand, as we have already argued, is

---

[91] In Shakespeare's time and accent, the first meaning of 'sullied' would have been 'solid', though the pun on 'sullied' in its contemporary meaning was certainly operative. Moreover, the pun represents another line of comparison between Lorenzo and Hamlet, as both are rather obsessed with what they see as the moral decline of those around them.

[92] Naomi Schor, 'La Pèrodie: superposition dans *Lorenzaccio*' in *Discours et pouvoir*, Ross Chambers (éd.) (Ann Arbor: University of Michigan, 1982), 78.

without landmarks. His injunction to kill a tyrant comes from nowhere, or rather from free-floating concerns in his reading and his culture. Even in the most nostalgic ritualised killing he can think to perform, Lorenzo is unable to verify anything. This distinction between Hamlet's and Lorenzo's experience of fatherlessness explains in part the different experiences of the two adolescents with respect to narrative and history.

Lorenzaccio clearly draws on *Hamlet* in its sweeping historical ambition. The number of characters, of scenes, of tableaux and especially the inclusion of bourgeois commentators at the edges of court life are innovations to French drama in the nineteenth century that trace their lineage to Shakespeare. Musset, like Shakespeare, attempts to show history in its moral and political complexity. Yet the heroes experience history very differently. Hamlet is not alone, but externally guided by his absent father and accompanied by Horatio who receives Hamlet's dying injunction to 'in this harsh world draw thy breath in pain, / To tell my story' (Act V, scene ii). Finally, Fortinbras' entrance and his command to 'Bear Hamlet like a soldier to the stage' elevates not just his body, but the events of the drama to historic proportions. Time was out of joint, and Hamlet, though haunted by this inherited responsibility 'was born to set it right' (Act I, scene v). Lorenzo, however, is either fatherless or has too many fathers. His story becomes no more than a *fait divers* as he disappears into the lagoon. 'Je ne nie pas l'histoire', he tells Philippe, 'mais je n'y étais pas.'[93] Lorenzo leaves either no one to tell his story or too many people to tell his story and nothing solid 'pas même un tombeau'[94] on which his story might be inscribed. Musset's *mise-en-scène* of history in *Lorenzaccio* reveals his intuition that history is not a clear narrative, but a chorus of chaotic whispers out of which we attempt to construct meaning.

This is one of the plays in Musset's œuvre most driven by nostalgia — the nostalgia of the Florentines for Republic, freedom, virtue and purity — but also a more generalised romantic nostalgia for verifiable values. Following the political upheavals beginning in 1789 and ending (at least for the moment) with 1830s uprising that failed to bring about any-

---

[93] Musset, *Théâtre*, 243.
[94] Ibid., 251.

thing substantive, this play about a Revolution that did not happen has to be taken to refer to contemporary French politics. The nostalgia for ritual, for transcendent truth in the sacrificial murder of the duke reflects onto the entire stage space. Again, in this nostalgia the stage and the altar are conflated as both the fictional realm of stage and its supposed referent, the altar, are put irremediably into question.

The three plays we have so far discussed in this chapter present characters trying to live out scripts or even write their own, unshakable in their belief in the power of narrative and performance to give them access to the sacred. In every case, however, the sacred shrinks to the dimensions of the book or the stage and the most access anyone gets to an 'outside' of absurdity is an unsustainable moment of belief in love, in happiness or in virtue. The need to use sacrifice as performance is a nostalgic urge backward towards the origins of religion, of theatre, of community and of the self. But the nostalgic stories told within the plays (Cœlio's mother's story, the childhood idyll of Perdican and Camille, the supposedly virtuous Florentine republic) all reveal the illusory nature of narrative. We never reach the site of origination, though we perhaps experience an illusory and vicarious glimpse of it in the performance of sacrifice — enough of a glimpse to keep us trying, never enough to satisfy us that it was real. We are either separated from the origin irreparably or perhaps there is no origin at all, only stories about the origin that must be told and retold.

Coda. A Compromise: Fantasio

In Chapter One we discussed plays in which, using theatrical techniques, characters arrive at some kind of substantiation of abstract claims shared by the stage world and the real world. The smooth operation of the system of exchange (which relies on the narrow correspondence between an abstract value and its concrete referent) is interrupted briefly by doubt; but in the end, sometimes with some remainder of uncertainty, the system is put back in order and continues to operate. In the second and third chapters we have so far focused on plays in a more pessimistic mode in which theatrical techniques fail utterly to provide proof; these plays end in violence, either willed and suicidal or random and incidental. Exchange either halts altogether as in *On ne badine pas avec l'amour,* or, as in *Lorenzaccio*, the system grinds on, despite Lorenzo's revelation of its fatal flaw (that the fictions of power and self are without referents); those in power capitalise precisely on the system's lack of substance in order to manipulate it and its participants.

On our way to a general conclusion, we will look at one last play by Alfred de Musset, the 1834 *Fantasio*, in which the characters come to a compromise of sorts between the two modes described above. On the one hand, *Fantasio* shares the daintiness and often a similarly formulaic subject matter with those we called 'proof plays;' on the other hand, similar to the other plays we have discussed, it foregrounds the volatility of the border between stage and world, where referentiality becomes inoperative. We argued before, that systems of exchange function because values are agreed upon, and, if confused or questioned, can be reaffirmed through performance or rejected and revised through violence. But the characters here manage to agree collectively to performances without proof, as the only value at the base of their system becomes a kind of innocent *joie de vivre*. The characters in *Fantasio* perform a complex negotiation between stage and world; while acknowledging what ought to be the border between the two, they choose to allow the fiction of the stage to have value in the world. Unlike Antony, Ruy Blas, or Lorenzo, who find only despair in the vulnerability of a world held together by fictions, the characters in this play find a limited kind of freedom in their indeterminate state; they find that playacting is enough.

Fantasio was first published in the *Revue des deux mondes* in January of 1834 but was not performed during the author's lifetime. Paul de Musset's rewriting of the play was produced in 1866 at the Comédie Française, but it was not until 1925 that *Fantasio* was performed in its original form. Like the plays discussed already in this chapter, *Fantasio* is the product of Musset's best two years (1833–1834) and is no less a masterpiece than *Lorenzaccio, Les Caprices de Marianne,* and *On ne badine pas avec l'amour.* The shortest of the four, *Fantasio* takes the examination of theatre, exchange, and subjectivity that we have discussed in the other plays considerably farther. Here, Fantasio's self-conscious meditations about the subject and about playing roles are contrasted with the unexamined doxa embodied by the prince. Finally, the artificial world of stage is chosen to the advantage of the heroes, but with ambiguous consequences to the community. The play opens on a compromise substantiated by an exchange, as the Bavarians celebrate the peace with Mantua which is to be consummated in the royal wedding of their princess Elsbeth with the prince of Mantua, their former enemy. In the opening scene, the king ponders the fairness of the exchange, wishing he could quantify the relative merits of the prince and his daughter. 'Dis moi, Rutten, tu as vu le prince; quel homme est-ce? Hélas! je lui donne ce que j'ai de plus précieux au monde, et je ne le connais point.'[95] The best the courtier can say, that 'le prince passe pour le meilleur des rois', is not enough. As an enemy the prince was at least a known quantity, but the sketchy approximation of his worth as a son-in-law and ally chagrins the king, who recognises the casualties of politics as well as those of war. 'La politique est une fine toile d'araignée, dans laquelle se débattent bien des pauvres mouches mutilées; je ne sacrifierai le bonheur de ma fille à aucun intérêt',[96] he concludes. Already, then, the play is questioning the supposed correspondence between the marriage exchange and its political counterpart: the exchange of peace for war, diplomacy for armed conflict.

Meanwhile, the prince is hatching a scheme to verify the agreement for himself. In the play's third scene he explains to his aide de camp: 'L'important projet que je médite est inouï dans ma famille; je prétends arriver à la cour du roi mon beau-père dans l'habillement d'un simple aide de camp ... je veux encore observer par mes yeux.'[97] Perhaps the plan is unheard of in his family, but of course, the exchange of coats and identities could not be more banal in the theatre and it sets up an expectation of a certain kind of comedy in which the essential value of the young lover in disguise will be recognised despite the costume. Yet the prince's insistence on the originality of his scheme is itself a source of comedy and allows us an already ironised view of his actions, especially in contrast to those of Fantasio. For not only is the prince's action unoriginal in the theatre in general, he is not even the first character in *this* play to de-

---

[95] Ibid., 104.
[96] Ibid.
[97] Ibid., 115.

cide to don a disguise. In the play's second scene, Fantasio, a young bourgeois bored with the insipidity of existence, decides to dress as the king's fool as a means of exploring another life. Fantasio wonders with pleasure, not fear, about the unknown; he longs to escape himself and his own interior space, which he knows only too well, in order to become 'ce monsieur qui passe'.[98] Fantasio muses:

> Je suis sûr que cet homme-là a dans la tête un millier d'idées qui me sont absolument étrangères; son essence lui est particulière. Hélas! tout ce que les hommes se disent entre eux se ressemble; les idées qu'ils échangent sont presque toujours les mêmes dans toutes leurs conversations; mais dans l'intérieur de ces machines isolées, quels replis, quels compartiments secrets! C'est tout un monde que chacun porte en lui! un monde ignoré qui naît et qui meurt en silence! Quelles solitudes que tous ces corps humains![99]

He is fundamentally sceptical about human intercourse, about exchange as anything more than empty formalism. He longs to go deeper into the human soul (for he does seem to believe in the soul, that 'essence particulière') to break through all the limits, physical and social, that separate people and to explode the barriers that create the solitude he loathes. Fantasio disguises himself as the king's fool not in order to prove something or stabilise something but to destabilise the social order that inhibits access to the other. His choice of the character of the fool is, of course, anything but gratuitous, for it is the fool who stands outside of social convention and who can speak the truth despite the strict social hierarchy that keeps the rest of the king's retinue subordinate. In the role of the fool, then, Fantasio explores something new, becomes something different and unknown to himself for the sake of that unknown, not, like the prince, to eliminate uncertainty.

Lorenzo, too, plays the fool and the comparison between the two most romantic of Musset's theatrical heroes is at least structurally apt, as both don disguises to insinuate themselves into a palace. More importantly, perhaps, both characters and both plays ask explicitly what makes a sub-

---

[98] Ibid., 108.
[99] Ibid.

ject. What would it mean for Fantasio to explore 'ce monsieur qui passe'? What would it mean for Lorenzo to become a Brutus? In *Lorenzaccio*, the hero's identity is the subject of much confusion and discussion among partisans of both sides of the political quarrel embroiling Florence. His ultimate failure to establish a coherent identity through performance or through narrative undermines the very category of identity and the concept of recognition itself. Lorenzo's quest, we argued, begins and ends with a fundamental alienation of the self that ultimately leads us to question whether there is anything but formal structure (disguise, roles, role models, stories, performances) to the subject. As we shall see, *Fantasio* also works against the idea of recognition in the parallel disguises of the prince (who is never recognised by the princess) and the hero (whose identity is ultimately rejected by her). Moreover, in *Fantasio* the question of the value of the individual is explicitly posed in the various characters' meditations on the upcoming royal wedding. The princess's fate — to be the sacrificial offering that will stop the war — is particularly poignant, and the play asks whether or not one can be asked to stand for many, what it means to the society to make such an exchange, and what it means for the princess to be their sacrificial lamb.

The disguises of Lorenzo and Fantasio allow them access to a world that would otherwise be beyond their reach. Literally for both characters this is the courtly space of political intrigue; but metaphorically, as Eric Gans has noted, both characters are figured as divers, going beneath the surface appearance of things to a deeper real.[100] Fantasio asks his friend Spark for a 'cloche de verre' so that he might explore the 'vaste Océan';[101] Lorenzo contrasts his fate with Philippe's, claiming: ' je me suis enfoncé dans cette mer houleuse de la vie; — j'en ai parcouru toutes les profondeurs, couvert de ma cloche de verre; — tandis que vous admiriez la surface, j'ai vu les débris des naufrages, les ossements et les Léviathans.'[102] Gans argues that Musset's divers (and he adds the heroes of *La Coupe et les lèvres* and *Les Marrons du feu*) hope to experience 'le

---

[100] Eric Gans, *Musset et le drame tragique* (Paris: José Corti, 1974), 143–66.
[101] Musset, *Théâtre*, 110.
[102] Ibid., 201.

réel dans sa vaste étendue'.[103] Lorenzo's quest, in particular, is 'une longue descente dans le réel où il fait connaissance intime avec les monstres'.[104] The characters are moving from a world of artifice to a realer world, what Gans calls the world of experience. Paradoxically, the site of experience is the interior site of introspection, which contrasts with the superficial, social exterior that is held together only by formal theatrical or narrative convention.

Gans's argument is in line with that of most critics, who generally view *Fantasio* as staging a conflict between a deeper real and a superficial world of artifice.[105] Critics often cite Fantasio's conversations with the princess in which he reproaches her for accepting a political marriage against her inclination. In the first scene of the second act Fantasio asks Elizabeth if a certain tulip is blue or red. When she replies confidently that it is blue, he questions her in a rather Socratic mode, arguing:

> Qui peut savoir sous le soleil s'il est né bleu ou rouge? Les tulipes elles-mêmes n'en savent rien. Les jardiniers et les notaires font des greffes si extraordinaires, que les pommes deviennent des citrouilles... Cette tulipe que voilà s'attendait bien à être rouge; mais on l'a mariée, elle est tout étonnée d'être bleue ... la pauvre dame Nature doit se rire parfois au nez de bon cœur, quand elle mire dans ses lacs et dans ses mers son éternelle mascarade.[106]

The world of society is the world of disguise, the anti-natural, artificial world. Fantasio seems to be advocating instead for a kind of natural personal integrity, an honesty that would go beyond and, in fact, run counter to what is required in social intercourse.

---

[103] Gans (1974), 148.
[104] Ibid., 161.
[105] Notably, David Sices argues that the play's conflict is between the real and what he terms the 'mechanical grotesque', and Rachel Wright argues that the play contrasts the artifice of an arranged marriage with real love. See the fourth chapter of David Sices, *Theatre of Solitude: the drama of Alfred de Musset* (Hanover: University Press of New England, 1974) and Rachel Wright, 'Male Reflectors in the Drama of Alfred de Musset', *French Review*, 65: 3 (February 1992), 393–401.
[106] Musset, *Théâtre*, 120.

While Gans and others are not wrong to point to a clear opposition between nature and artifice set up in Fantasio's conversations with the princess, they fail to interrogate sufficiently the terms of the discussion. The question of artifice and the real quickly becomes muddied when we consider that it is only through artifice (disguise, acting) that Fantasio has access to the so-called 'real'. In fact, we are dealing with two different movements within the play: a nostalgic movement toward a pure nature, and a humanistic or individualistic movement that might lead to a privileged space beyond nature. On the one hand, in Fantasio's discourse on the tulip quoted above, he bemoans the corruption of Nature, in a sort of romantic Platonism that sees the hand of man as a degrading force. This represents a nostalgia that pulls the hero backward towards a pure, essential, ideal state. At the same time, however, the play presents a different discourse about nature, as the hero's ennui in the second scene of the play extends beyond the social world to implicate even the natural world: 'Comme ce soleil couchant est manqué! La nature est pitoyable ce soir. ... Je faisais des paysages comme celui-là quand j'avais douze ans, sur la couverture de mes livres de classe'.[107] Artifice, even the presumably poor sketches of a child, is here seen as the equal of a Nature that has lost the charm of novelty. Through artifice (his disguise) Fantasio will attempt to go beyond not only social convention but also the known natural world.[108]

The musings of Lorenzo and Fantasio seem to say that there is a hidden depth of reality, which is inaccessible without some romantic epiphany or theatrical *rite de passage*. As Lorenzo plays the role of the vicious courtier, he achieves a sort of second sight, allowing him to see beyond the disguises of others: 'tous les masques tombaient devant mon regard.'[109] However, what he sees behind those masks is the omnipresence

---

[107] Ibid., 108.
[108] This is quite similar to Diderot's argument about acting in 'Le Paradoxe sur le comédien'. He argues that the better actor is the one who is guided by judgment and cold reason and not by sensitivity and emotion. The better actor is not 'really feeling' the emotions he is expressing, but imitating them through observation, craft and practice.
[109] Musset, *Théâtre*, 202.

of vice, figured throughout the play in terms of instability, femininity, promiscuity and infection. The truer realm into which only Lorenzo can see is revealed to be no different from (or perhaps worse than) the corrupt 'artificial' world of the court. Moreover, Lorenzo is transformed by this discovery, such that when he wants to lay aside his disguise and resume his previously virtuous existence he cannot. 'Le vice a été pour moi un vêtement; maintenant, il est collé à ma peau.'[110] There is, finally, no outside of disguise, nothing deeper beneath appearances. This same movement in *Fantasio*, by which the masked figure succeeds in unmasking (or in this case, unwigging) the other, is not a sign of a degrading and ubiquitous corruption; rather, Fantasio represents an optimistic possibility for the role of the artist. While recognising the nostalgic urge towards a past of lost unity, he is not fooled by it, but in the role of the fool, goes forward toward an ideal of Art.

Unlike Lorenzo, Fantasio maintains a distinction between self and disguise, between the world in which he lives and the world in which he performs. The relationship between them, however, is anything but simple. Generally in theatre we understand there to be a relationship of referentiality between stage and world: the artificial stage space stands in temporarily for the real world of the spectators and the audience makes the necessary psychological association to apply conclusions from the stage to their lives. This argument about theatre is analogous to the argument made by all of the sacrifice thinkers about the ritual sacrifice. Through the theatrical performance or the performance of sacrifice, the spectators associate the physical reality of the stage or the physical body of the sacrificial victim with some abstract notion (such as community, continuity or the realness of God). The audience in the theatre and the witnesses to sacrifice enact meaning similarly, then, through an association of the physical component of the spectacle with the abstract ideas that they seek to substantiate in their lives. In *Fantasio* we might argue after Gans that the relationship between stage and world is merely inverted intact: the stage space (the princess's garden) where Fantasio plays his role becomes the site of 'real' experience, while life in the external space of court or city is

---

[110] Ibid., 203.

merely the degraded form of the goings-on in that privileged interior. We are meant to learn the simple, romantic lesson that the introspective individual may be an outcast of society, but that he belongs to a better society, made up of those who see beyond the empty formalism of commonplace social interactions. This is the lesson, we argued in Chapter One, of *Antony*, *Chatterton*, and to some extent *Kean*. Still, in those plays, the establishment of the referential relationship between stage and world, whether inverted or not, required physical presence, bodies that proved something, and *Fantasio* refuses authentication at every turn. The movement forward that Fantasio is attempting to enact, through Art to the ideal space beyond everyday life and the everyday experience of Nature, is both unsubstantiatable and unsustainable.

The prince's role-reversal with his lieutenant and his relationship to Fantasio illustrate what I have just alluded to as the play's refusal of authentication. The prince is, as mentioned earlier, attempting to arrive at proof through performance. His playacting runs parallel to Fantasio's: they are set up as rivals for the attention of the princess as both try to tease her real feelings out of her (although it turns out that Fantasio is not interested in a romantic relationship with her). Even in the prank that puts the prince into conflict with Fantasio (Fantasio's unwigging of the prince) the two characters will not meet in a direct confrontation: first of all it is not seen on-stage, but recounted in Act II, scene vi; next, it is not really the prince, but Marinoni in the prince's coat whose wig is removed, and finally the prince's anger is doubly mediated through Marinoni, who plays the role of the prince, and through the king, who imprisons Fantasio at the prince's / Marinoni's request. From prison, Fantasio summarises: 'Voilà le mariage manqué et tout remis en question. Le prince de Mantoue a demandé ma tête, en échange de sa perruque.'[111] When the prince's performance fails, he loses all perspective and embarks on a mission not unlike that of Hugo's Triboulet, as his urge to destroy what he cannot control gets the better of him. He finally leaves the Bavarian court (and the stage) without ever having been recognised by the courtiers and without ever recognising his own folly. For although the play sets up a kind of

[111] Ibid., 132.

mirror game with the prince and Fantasio, it refuses the moment of recognition by which the prince might come to see himself in the fool, and the prince thus fails to correct his behaviour.[112] The play on theatrical convention that characterises so much of Musset's work leads to another unusual conclusion. Arnaud Tripet notes that in traditional comedies where pairs of masters and servants are in disguise, a source of comedy is often the servant's difficulty in imitating the master's more refined manners. In *Fantasio*, however, 'celui qui est ridicule ... est le titré, et celui qui est le maître du ridicule est le bouffon ... L'aisance n'est plus, dans ce cadre, affaire de rang ni de bienséance, mais d'esprit'.[113] Traditional comedy takes as a given that the servant imitates the master and that there is a direct correspondence between birth and ability.[114] Musset shifts the mirrors, such that Fantasio and the prince are not modelled one after the other but represent different models of acting; this is underscored by the fact that Fantasio is not the prince's servant and the role played by the prince's servant is minimal. The prince gives himself up passively and blindly to conventions to which he never really commits himself: on two different occasions he is prepared to change coats with Marinoni and reassume his real identity, but finally decides to remain in disguise. He defers the moment of recognition until he misses it altogether, unable to find the way out of the role he has assumed. Fantasio, on the other hand, takes the job of fool only to allay his boredom. 'Il n'y a point de maître d'armes mélancolique',[115] he tells Spark and promptly sets himself to work. Still, even though Fantasio performs well, his performance does not guarantee the resolution we expect from a com-

[112] The happy resolution of a 'proof play' often depends on a character's coming around to an understanding of his or her faults. See, for example, our discussion of *Un Caprice* in Chapter One.
[113] Arnaud Tripet, 'Préface' to his edition of *Fantasio* (Paris: Librairie Générale Française, 1993), 45–46.
[114] Even in *Ruy Blas*, which questions this correspondence, Hugo leaves open the possibility that Ruy Blas is not entirely common. We are told that he and Don César ressemble each other as two brothers, thus implying that they are half-brothers and that Ruy Blas does carry (though, he himself is illegitimate) noble blood.
[115] Musset, *Théâtre*, 109.

edy. If Fantasio's role-playing is responsible for the prevention of the 'wrong' marriage, it does not lead to an alternate marriage for the princess. The marriage ceremony or the profession of love which we have argued elsewhere is the substantiating act that eliminates indeterminacy and underscores the function of theatre (to anchor abstract values) never takes place. Instead, violence is unleashed in the coming war while Fantasio and the princess pledge only their friendship. The princess remains in her garden, unscathed but unattached.

In the play's last scene, the princess sees Fantasio without the disguise of the fool and wonders whether he might really be the prince. This briefly opens the possibility of a romantic relationship between Fantasio and Elsbeth because she thinks she has found her correct mate in the handsome young man for whom she has such obvious affinity. When Fantasio finally reveals his identity, the princess rejects it, refusing to recognise him as himself and commanding him: 'ne parais jamais devant moi sans cette taille contrefaite et ces grelots d'argent ... tu redeviendras mon bouffon pour le temps qu'il te plaira de l'être, et puis tu iras à tes affaires.'[116] Though he somehow remains 'himself', it is only armed with the key to the garden and the costume of a fool that Fantasio has access to the other's interior space, the space he longed to discover in his first conversation with Spark. Though it is here, in the princess's garden, that Fantasio has found real feeling and in his relationship to the princess some kind of true (though Platonic) love, this world of the other is finally not a deeper real than that of his everyday life, only a real apart. In this way, Fantasio's movement forward to an ideal of art succeeds only conditionally. While he refuses the princess's offer to be paid for his acting, his new status is sustained only by his agreement with the princess. 'J'aime ce métier plus que tout autre; mais je ne puis faire aucun métier.'[117] Refusing the reality of Fantasio's identity, the princess strikes a bargain with Fantasio to maintain her belief in what is not, and it is that private convention (they pretend he is deformed and deranged) and not physical real-

---

[116] Ibid., 136.
[117] Ibid., 135.

ity (he is actually a handsome and intelligent young man) that will determine their relationship.

The Gouvernante witnesses but is left out of Elsbeth and Fantasio's *folie à deux*. The Gouvernante shows herself to be aware of the theatrical aspects of the events at court through references she makes on different occasions, always using the rhetorical figure of antonomasia. In Act II, scene one, she refers to St. Jean as 'un vrai Triboulet',[118] and in Act II, scene five, she calls the prince 'un véritable Almaviva',[119] the count in disguise in Beaumarchais's *Barbier de Séville*. At first she seems to model the correct audience response to the play, as she astutely matches the events of the play to their external, theatrical referents. In the end, however, the Gouvernante is revealed to be an ineffective spectator; the last word of the play is hers as she wonders how she could have missed the prince: 'Est-il possible que le prince de Mantoue soit parti sans que je l'aie vu?'[120] The moment of recognition never comes; physical reality is obscured by disguise and then disguise is maintained in the place of identity. The rules of the theatre are extended to the world, as disguise becomes the rule and not the privileged exception that substantiates some underlying rule about the world.

If art succeeds conditionally in uniting the princess with Fantasio, the other movement traced in the play, the nostalgia for a pure ideal, fails utterly. Here, as in *Lorenzaccio*, Musset's romantic nostalgia goes beyond the regret of the fall of Man, which might be overcome in some Hugolian progress of the human spirit. Different from Lorenzo, however, the princess and Fantasio find liberty and not despair in the lack of references. The characters choose to divorce their play space from the outside world, and the correspondence between idea and object ceases to be relevant in the privileged space of the princess's garden. The way back to the supposedly pure origin is lost, but not tragically, for the search for it is simply abandoned, as the characters discover that their collusion is enough to sustain the world as they would like it to be.

---

[118] Ibid., 118.
[119] Ibid., 129.
[120] Ibid., 136,

But what about the world beyond the princess's garden? The political dilemma on which the play opens is lost temporarily in the *marivaudage* of the second act and is reintroduced only in the threat of the coming war. The princess's marriage was meant to prevent the war and save the community, but her private agreement with Fantasio supersedes that abstract relationship. In the Gouvernante's words, the princess is 'un vrai agneau pascal',[121] already a substitute victim taking the place of the many who would die in war, and it seems at first that, like Iphigeneia, only another substitute victim will save her. In a way, Fantasio is that substitute victim, and while we cannot take Fantasio seriously as a Christ figure, there are some facts we cannot deny. Like Christ, Fantasio follows St. Jean; he then lowers himself to the state of fool to rise again to his own identity at the play's conclusion. The princess and her Gouvernante visit him in the jail like the Marys at the tomb and witness his transformation. On two occasions, Fantasio is explicitly compared to Christ: in his first conversation with Spark he declares, 'Je danse comme Jésus-Christ sur le vaste Océan';[122] when the Gouvernante sees him in prison without his disguise she exclaims, 'Il est beau comme un vrai Jésus.'[123] Yet the differences and inversions in Fantasio and Christ are perhaps more telling: instead of standing in for the suffering of all, Fantasio does not really suffer. Christ comes to free the captives and Fantasio does free the princess, but she frees him quite literally in return. A kind of reciprocation or collusion forms the basis of their relationship and undermines any kind of transcendent function Fantasio might have fulfilled as sacrificial victim because his role does not extend beyond the princess's locked garden.

Fantasio plays with the idea of sacrifice, of proof, of Christ figures and in the end turns them all around to the reserved use of two individuals. The war will come, but not to the princess's garden. Like *Lorenzaccio*, which tells the story of a revolution that did not happen, *Fantasio* is the story of a non-event. The royal wedding does not take place; the truce fails to sustain itself; the prince comes and goes without ever being recognised. But somehow, despite the wars and the prisons and the deaths of

[121] Ibid., 117.
[122] Ibid., 110.
[123] Ibid., 133.

many fools, this diaphanous play seems to say that the will to believe in fantasy is sustenance enough. Rather than coming to some sort of proof about the world made possible by the intercession of the stage, Fantasio manages to do the opposite, to make his corner of the world refer to the stage by the evacuation of physical proof.

Conclusion

The theatrical performance gives a concrete form to the abstract contents of the theatrical text, and then is interpreted by the audience as the concrete representation of abstract values — those announced in the text and those espoused by the audience members in their lives. Throughout this volume I have attempted to show how theatre functions according to Elaine Scarry's principle of analogical verification. The physical stage is understood to lend reality to the abstract idea, and so in the acting out of anxieties the community attempts to exorcise them from their midst, leaving only the solid representation of the values that bind them. Indeed the origins of theatre in the ritual sacrifice lend credence to our association of Scarry's principle with the theatre, but ultimately, the verification enacted (whether in theatre or, as Scarry describes it, in war) does not hold, but must be repeated *ad infinitum*. In the theatre as in life, the relationship between abstract idea and concrete manifestation — a relationship negotiated by the intermediary principle of performance — is complex, oblique and shifting. In focusing on plays that question the principle of performance by presenting characters who, within the play, are performing roles or trying themselves to arrive at some kind of analogical verification, I have attempted to chart the possible effects of performance. I have shown that rather than substantiating abstract ideas, some plays actually stage the collapse of the supposed correspondence between stage and world. Finally, the abstract values whose substantiation is withheld are revealed to be no less the product of human imagining than the fictions enacted on stage.

The first chapter examined plays by Alfred de Musset, Alfred de Vigny and Alexandre Dumas, *père* in the most traditional mode, in which values are eventually substantiated and doubt for the most part eradicated. The second chapter analysed three plays by Victor Hugo, cases in which performance tends toward violence; but instead of a foundational or purifying violence, which, so the story goes, strengthens a community, violence here is random and suicidal and leads only to dissolution. The third chapter dealt with four plays by Musset in which performances evoke the ritual sacrifice and therefore the origins of theatre. The first three of these plays stage the failure of the individual or of the community to enact meaning and in the last play, *Fantasio*, meaning is dodged, as characters give up the idea of transcendent or permanent truth and settle for the limited truth that theatre provides.

Even while delving into the specifics of the different plays, I have tried to study the structure of theatre in general as much as a study of French Romantic theatre in particular. While, as I have attempted to show, the specific concerns of Romantic theatre can be contextualised historically in the anxieties populating the *zeitgeist* of France in the 1830s, I have not tried to define or develop an argument about their historical specificity. I have, in fact, focused on elements of this theatre that are far from unique to it. In this way, my argument has been about theatre itself and how it functions in culture, about performance itself and how it functions in theatre and in our lives. If performance is, as I have argued throughout, a basic element of the structure of belief in our culture, then understanding performance is essential to understanding our collective inability to get beyond the limiting and unsubstantiatable myths of our culture.

Still, my choice of French Romantic theatre was not arbitrary, for the thirteen plays discussed in this volume were all written following a period of extensive reflection on the purpose and the process of theatre. Moreover, the reflection on theatre extends beyond the prefaces and pamphlets and finds expression in the plays themselves, whose theatricality lays bare the structure of performance. What strikes me about the debates on Romantic theatre is how much they mattered to the writers and thinkers of the period. This can partly be explained by market forces: writers in the 1830s could make money with novels, but the theatre is where the real money could be made and the theatre was certainly the best way to reach a large number of people and to solidify a literary reputation. In French culture, the most admired writers are even today the great playwrights: Corneille, Racine, Molière, and all of the important writers of the nineteenth century attempted, with mixed success, to write plays. So it mattered to the playwrights of the period that the kinds of plays each camp — the Romantics and the neo-classicists — wanted to write be recognised and performed. While the Comédie Française finally caved in to these market pressures and allowed the *drame romantique* to take its hallowed stage, the Académie Française kept up the theoretical battle against the dramatic reform. Remember it was the then fledgling Académie that had argued against Corneille in the *Querelle du Cid* in 1638, and many of the debates were the same: what is *vraisemblance*? what is the role of the audience? in what form can we best express contemporary themes? And most of all, what is the definition of theatre? The most humorous section of Stendhal's *Racine et Shakespeare* deals significantly with a parodic session of the Académie in which the members try to define 'romanticism' for the official dictionary of French.

As this study has shown, the plays themselves reflect this contemporary concern with the form and function of theatre in culture. While the plays studied here are all products of the 'major' playwrights of the period, some are minor works, which have as yet attracted little critical attention. If I have chosen to include a discussion of these lesser plays in this volume, it was in part to show that the contemporary fascination with performance was more widespread than the rarefied realms of high culture. Considering all of these texts from the angle of performance studies has, I hope, shed new light on performance as both structure and theme in the Romantic theatre, but more importantly, I hope to have laid the groundwork for further study of the vast production of popular, 'non-canonical' plays of this period.

I have suggested that theatrical performance is only one of a variety of ways that societies or even different segments of one society work out the dissonance involved in the fragmentation of culture. It is my hope that this study of performance in a specific moment in theatre will provide a framework through which we can see the limits and the power of performances of all kinds in the ongoing process of meaning-making, which is the work of culture.

Bibliography

Complete references to the works cited in this volume are provided in the footnotes that accompany each chapter. The present bibliography is offered as an overview to the major texts of performance theory as well as to the major critical studies of the romantic theatre of the last half-century or so. Lists of key editions and of critical studies for each of the authors treated in this volume also follow.

Romantic Theatre and the Romantic Period

Abraham, Pierre (ed.), *Manuel d'histoire littéraire de la France* (Paris: Éditions sociales, 1972), IV.

Affron, Charles, *A Stage for Poets: studies in the theatre of Hugo and Musset* (Princeton: Princeton University Press, 1971).

Amono, Reginald F., 'Corneille et les Romantiques' in *Actes du Colloque tenu à Rouen du 2 au 6 octobre 1984*, ed. Alain Niderst (Paris: Presses Universitaires de France, 1985), 27–32.

Barbéris, Pierre, *Prélude à l'utopie* (Paris: Presses Universitaires de France, 1991).

Bowman, Frank, 'Notes Toward the Definition of the Romantic Theater', *L'Ésprit Créateur*, 5: 3 (Fall 1965), 121–30.

Brooks, Peter, *The Melodramatic Imagination* (New Haven and London: Yale University Press, 1976; repr. 1995).

Carlson, Marvin, 'The French Censorship Enquiries of 1849 and 1891', *Essays in Theatre*, 5: 1 (Nov 1986), 5.

Cooper, Barbara, 'Toward a Semiotic Description of French Historical Dramas of the Early Nineteenth Century', *Nineteenth-Century French Studies*, 13: 2–3 (Winter–Spring 1985), 74–84.

Degranges, Charles-Marc, *La Presse littéraire sous la Restauration* (Paris: Mercure de France, 1907).

Denommé, Robert T., 'Chatterton, Ruy Blas, Lorenzaccio: three tragic heroes', *Laurels*, 61 (Spring 1990), 55–67.

Descotes, Maurice, *Le Public de Théâtre et son histoire* (Paris: Presses Universitaires de France, 1964).

——, *Historique de la critique dramatique en France* (Tubingen: Gunter Nurr Verlag, 1980).

Houssaye, Arsène, *Les Confessions* (Paris: Dentu, 1885).

Howarth, W.D., *Sublime and Grotesque: a study of French Romantic drama* (London: Harrap, 1975)

——, 'Drama' in *The French Romantics*, ed. D.G. Charlton (Cambridge: Cambridge University Press, 1984), 205–47.

Jomaron, Jacqueline de, (éd.), *Le Théâtre en France* (Paris: Armand Colin, 1992).

Krakovitch, Odile, 'Les Romantiques et la censure au théâtre', *Revue d'Histoire du Théâtre*, 36: 1 (Jan–Mar 1984), 68.

Stendhal, *Racine et Shakespeare* (Paris: Garnier-Flammarion, 1970).

Thomasseau, Jean-Marie, *Le Mélodrame* (Paris: Presses Universitaires de France, 1984).

Ubersfeld, Anne, *Le Drame romantique* (Paris: Belin Sup, 1993).

Performance Theory and Literary Theory

Arnold, Paul, *L'Avenir du théâtre* (Paris: Savel, 1947).

Artaud, Antonin, *Le Théâtre et son double* (Paris: Gallimard, 1964).

Austin, John L., *How to Do Things with Words* (Cambridge: Harvard University Press, 1962).

Bakhtine, Mikhaïl, *L'Œuvre de François Rabelais et la culture populaire au moyen âge et sous la renaissance*, tr. Andrée Robel (Paris: Gallimard, 1970).

——, *Toward a Philosophy of the Act*, tr. Vadim Liapunov (Austin: University of Texas Press, 1993).

Barnouw, Erik, *International Encyclopedia of Communications* (New York: Oxford University Press, 1987).

Bataille, Georges, *L'Érotisme* (Paris: Éditions de Minuit, 1957).

——, *Œuvres complètes, Premiers Écrits (1922–1940)* (Paris: Gallimard, 1970).

——, *Œuvres complètes*, 9 vols (Paris: Gallimard 1979).

Brecht, Bertolt, *Brecht on Theatre*, ed. and tr. John Willet (New York: Hill and Wang, 1964).

Carlson, Marvin, *Performance: a critical introduction* (London and New York: Routledge, 1996).

Cavell, Stanley, *Must We Mean What We Say?* (Cambridge: Cambridge University Press, 1976).

——, *Disowning Knowledge in Six Plays of Shakespeare* (Cambridge, Cambridge University Press, 1987).

Coppieters, Frank, 'Performance and Perception', *Poetics Today*, 2: 3 (Spring 1981), 35–48.

Derrida, Jacques, *L'Écriture et la différence* (Paris: Éditions du Seuil, 1967).

Diderot, Denis, *Paradoxe sur le comédien* (Paris: Garnier-Flammarion, 1967).

Durand, Régis, *La Relation théâtrale* (Lille: Presses Universitaires de Lille, 1980).

Durkheim, Émile, *Les Formes elementaires de la vie religieuse: Le système totémique en Australie* (Paris: Presses Universitaires de France, 5e ed., 1968).

Girard, René, *La Violence et le sacré* (Paris: Éditions du monde, 1972).

Issacharoff, Michael, 'Space and Reference in Drama', *Poetics Today*, 2: 3 (Spring 1981), 211–24.

Larthomas, P., *Le Langage dramatique* (Paris: Presses Universitaires de France, 1980).

Mauss, Marcel, *Sociologie et anthropologie* (Paris: Presses Universitaires de France, 1973).

Nietzsche, Friedrich, *Birth of Tragedy*, tr. Walter Kaufmann (New York: Vintage Books, 1967).

Parker, Andrew and Eve Kosofsky Sedgwick (eds), *Performativity and Performance* (New York: Routledge, 1995).

Pavis, Patrice, *Languages of the Stage* (New York: Performing Arts Journal Publications, 1982).

Phelan, Peggy and Jill Lane (eds), *The Ends of Performance* (New York: New York University Press, 1998).

Pontbriand, Chantal, 'The Eye finds no fixed point on which to rest...' *Modern Drama*, 25 (1982), 154–62.

Przybos, Julia, 'Melodrama as Social Ritual', *Theater and Society in French Literature*, French Literature Series, vol. 25 (Columbia: University of South Carolina, 1988), 86–94.

Reinelt, Janelle G. and Joseph R. Roach, *Critical Theory and Performance* (Ann Arbor: University of Michigan Press, 1992).

Salyer, Jeffrey William, 'The Expressionist Stage in Light of Bataillian Expenditure', Dissertation presented at the University of Washington, 1999.

Scarry, Elaine, *The Body in Pain* (New York: Oxford University Press, 1985).

Schechner, Richard and Willa Appel (eds), *By Means of Performance* (Cambridge: Cambridge University Press, 1990).

Schechner, Richard, *Performance Theory* (New York and London: Routledge, 1988).

States, Bert O., *Great Reckonings in Little Rooms* (Berkeley: University of California Press, 1987).

Steiner, George, *The Death of Tragedy* (London: Faber and Faber, 1961).

Turner, Victor, *Le Phénomène rituel*, tr. Gérard Guillet (Paris: Presses Universitaires de France, 1990).

Alexandre Dumas

Bassan, Fernande et Sylvie Chevalley, *Alexandre Dumas, père et la Comédie-Française* (Paris: Minard, 1972).

Bassan, Fernande, 'Dumas père et le drame romantique', *L'Esprit Créateur*, 5: 3 (Fall 1965), 174–8.

Dumas, Alexandre. *Théâtre complet* (Paris: Colman Lévy, 1889), V.

——, *Mes Mémoires* (Paris: Gallimard, 1967).

——, *Drames romantiques*, ed. Claude Aziza (Paris: Omnibus, 2002).

——, *Antony*, ed. Pierre-Louis Rey (Paris: Gallimard, 2002).

——, *Antony* (Paris: Éditions de la Table Ronde, 1994).

——, *Antony*, ed. Joseph Varro (Paris: Larousse, 1970).

Hemmings, F.W.J., *Alexandre Dumas: the king of romance* (New York: Charles Scribner's Sons, 1979).

McCall, Dorothy, *The Theatre of Jean-Paul Sartre* (New York: Columbia University Press, 1967).

Schopp, Claude, *Alexandre Dumas* (Paris: Fayard, 2002 (Paris: Mazarine for first edition, 1985).

Ubersfeld, Anne, 'Alexandre Dumas, père, et le drame bourgeois', *Cahiers de l'Association internationale des études françaises*, 35 (mai 1983), 121–39.

Victor Hugo

Chahine, Samia, *La Dramaturgie de Victor Hugo* (Paris: Éditions A.-G. Nizet, 1971).

Claudon, Francis (ed.), *Le Rayonnement international de Victor Hugo* (New York: Peter Lang, 1989).

Cooper, Barbara, 'Parodying Hugo', *European Romantic Review*, 2: 1 (Summer 1991), 23–38.

Gaudon, Jean, 'Sur *Hernani*', *Cahiers de l'Association internationale des études françaises*, 35 (mai 1983), 101–20.

Hugo, Victor, *Théâtre complet* (Paris: Gallimard, 1963), I.

Moors, Daniel, 'Second Empire France in the Allegorical Mirror: the meeting of 'Theater' and 'Society' in Victor Hugo's *L'Épée* (1869)', *Theater and Society in French Literature*, French Literature Series, 25 (Columbia: University of South Carolina, 1988), 58–67.

Ubersfeld, Anne, *Le Roi et le bouffon: Étude sur le théâtre de Hugo de 1830 à 1839* (Paris: Librairie José Corti, 1974).

Alfred de Musset

Alexandre, Didier, 'Florence extra muros: remarques sur l'espace dans *Lorenzaccio', Littérature,* 23 (Fall 1990), 117–34.

Amossy, Ruth, *Carnaval et comédie dans* Les Caprices de Marianne *d'Alfred de Musset* (Paris: Minard, 1973).

——, 'Towards a Rhetoric of the Stage: the scenic realization of verbal clichés', *Poetics Today,* 2: 3 (Spring 1981), 49–63.

Bedner, Jules, 'Sur les intrigues du théâtre de Musset', *Revue des Sciences Humaines,* 41: 162 (1976), 271–98.

——, *'Lorenzaccio* ou *Œdipe* à « Florence »', Neophilologus 24: 1 (1983), 42–54.

Bem, Jeanne, *'Lorenzaccio* entre l'histoire et le fantasme', *Poétique,* 11: 44 (nov. 1980), 451–61.

——, *Le Texte traversé* (Paris: Honoré Champion, 1991).

Chevalley, Sylvie, 'Musset à la Comédie-Française', *Europe* (nov.–déc. 1977), 17–39.

Chotard, Loïc, 'Le Théâtre à l'essai', in *Musset*: Lorenzaccio, On ne badine pas avec l'amour, ed. Michel Crouzet (Paris: SEDES, 1990), 25–43.

Cooper, Barbara, 'Staging a Revolution', *Romance Notes,* 24: 1 (1983), 23–29.

——, 'Breaking Up / Down / Apart: "L'Eclatement" as a Unifying Principle in Musset's *Lorenzaccio', Philological Quarterly,* 65: 1 (Winter 1986), 103–12.

——, 'Il faut suivre votre modèle', *French Literature Series, Columbia, SC* 15 (1988), 95–108.

Creignou, Pierre, 'Petite suite sur *Fantasio', Europe,* 583–4 (1977), 87–96.

Dauphiné, James, 'Le masque dans *Lorenzaccio', Europe* (nov.–déc 1977), 61–68.

Denommé, Robert T., 'The Motif of the « Poète Maudit » in Musset's *Lorenzaccio', L'Esprit Créateur,* 5: 3 (Fall 1965), 138–46.

Dessons, Gérard, 'La parole du siècle dans les Proverbes de Musset', *Travaux de Littérature,* 4 (1991), 197–207.

Diaz, José Luis, 'Le Corps et le signe', Littérature, 31 (oct. 1978), 43–63.

——, *Lorenzaccio* (Paris: Cahiers Textuels Paris 7, 1991).

Didier, Jean-Jacques, *L'Esprit: Stylistique du mot d'esprit dans le théâtre de Musset* (Amsterdam: Rodopi, 1992).

Donnard, J.-H., '*L'Âne et le ruisseau*, proverbe imité de Carmontelle', *Revue des Sciences Humaines* (oct.–déc. 1962), 621–6.

Duchet, Claude, 'Une dramaturgie de la parole', in *Journées d'études sur Alfred de Musset* (Clermont-Ferrand: Société des Études Romantiques, 1978), 49–62.

Fabig, Angelika, *Kunst und Künstler im Werk Alfred de Mussets* (Heidleberg: Carl Winter–Universitätsverlag, 1976).

Fairchild, Sharon, 'Les Personnages de femmes dans huit pièces de Musset', *Nineteenth Century French Studies*, 4: 3 (1976), 213–19.

Gamble, Donald, 'Developing Drama: the earliest Contes en vers of Alfred de Musset', *Dalhousie French Studies*, 12 (Spring-Summer 1798), 3–18.

——, ' The Image of Italy in the Creative Imagination of Alfred de Musset' in *Space and Boundaries in Literature*, ed. Roger Bauer (Munich: Iudicium 1990), 305–11.

——, 'Alfred de Musset and the Uses of Experience', *Nineteenth-Century French Studies*, 18: 1–2 (Fall–Winter 1989–1990), 78–84.

Gans, Eric L., *Musset et le 'Drame tragique'* (Paris: Librairie José Corti, 1974).

Gaudard, François-Charles, 'Introduction à la lecture de *On ne badine pas avec l'amour*', *Champs du Signe:Cahiers de Stylistique*, 1 (1991), 149–61.

Gochberg, Herbert S., *Stage of Dreams: the dramatic art of Alfred de Musset* (Geneva: Droz, 1967).

Hamilton, James F., 'Mimetic Desire in Musset's *Lorenzaccio*', *Romance Quarterly*, 32: 4 (1985), 347–57.

Heyvaert, Alain, *La Transparence et l'indicible dans l'œuvre d'Alfred de Musset* (Paris: Klincksieck, 1994).

——, *L'Esthétique de Musset* (Paris: SEDES, 1996).

Jeune, Simon, *Musset et sa fortune littéraire* (Bordeaux: G. Ducros, 1970).

——, '*Lorenzaccio*, drame romantique?' in *Journées d'études sur Alfred de Musset* (Clermont-Ferrand: Société des Études Romantiques, 1978), 108–25.

——, 'Musset auteur féministe?' *Travaux de Linguistique et de* Littérature, 21: 2 (1983), 43–55.

Johnson, Warren, 'Capricious Exuberance: Gender and Mediation in Musset's Comedies', *Dalhousie French Studies*, 33 (Winter 1995), 27–34.

Kirton, W.J.S., 'The Importance of Family in *Lorenzaccio*', *Trivium*, 12 (1978), 125–34.

Kraus, Kenneth, 'Lorenzaccio, Castraccio, Lorenzetta: a consideration of who may play Musset's Lorenzo', *George Sand Studies*, 10: 1–2 (1990–1991), 18–27.

Kupisz, Kazimierz, 'Les Doubles et dédoublements de l'amour (Louise Labé, Marivaux, Musset)', in *Doubles et dédoublement en littératur*, éd. Gabriel Perouse (Saint Étienne: Université de Saint Étienne, 1995), 77–90.

Labarre, Françoise, 'De Terence à Pirandello: La Comédie gaie', *L'Information Littéraire*, 36: 1 (1984), 35–37.

Larthomas, P., 'Un problème de mise en scène', in *Journées d'études sur Alfred de Musset* (Clermont-Ferrand: Société des Études Romantiques, 1978), 126–35.

Leach, Laurie, 'Lorenzo and the Noblest Roman', *Romance Notes*, 28: 3 (1988), 241–5.

Le Roux, Monique, 'Début de saison à la Comédie Française', *La Quinzaine Littéraire*, 543 (16–30 nov. 1989), 26–27.

Lieber, Gérard, 'À propos de la mise en scène des *Caprices* par Baty', in *Journées d'études sur Alfred de Musset* (Clermont-Ferrand: Société des Études Romantiques, 1978), 93–96.

Lowin, Joseph, 'The Frames of *Lorenzaccio*', *French Review*, 53: 2 (1979), 190–98.

MacInnes, John W., '*Lorenzaccio* and the Drama of Narration' in *Text and Presentation: The University of Florida Department of Classics Comparative Drama Conference Papers*, VIII, ed. Karelisa Hartigan (Lanham: University Press of America, 1988), 137–45.

MacLean, Marie, 'The Sword and the Flower: the sexual symbolism of *Lorenzaccio*', *Australian Journal of French Studies*, 16: 2 (1979), 166–81.

Malachy, Thérèse, 'Du Meurtre politique au sacrifice rituel', *Revue d'Histoire du théâtre*, 40: 3 (1988), 273–80.

Malthus, Cecil, *Musset et Shakespeare: étude analytique de l'influence de Shakespeare sur le théâtre d'Alfred de Musset* (New York: Peter Lang, c. 1988).

Masson, Bernard, 'Le Masque, le double et la personne dans quelques *Comédies et proverbes'*, *Revue des sciences humaines*, 107 (oct.–déc. 1962), 551–71.

——, *Musset et son double: lecture de Lorenzaccio* (Paris: Librairie Minard, 1978).

——, *Lectures de l'imaginaire* (Paris: Presses Universitaires de France, 1993).

Mauzi, Robert, 'Les Fantoches d'Alfred de Musset', *Revue d'Histoire littéraire de la France*, 66 (1966). 257–82.

McCready, Susan, 'The Secret Self: a reading of Musset's *André del Sarto*', *Nineteenth-Century French Studies*, forthcoming.

——, Power and Sexual Congress in Alfred de Musset's *Lorenzaccio'*, *Romance Notes*, 44: 1 (Fall 2003), 83–91.

——, 'Performing Stability: The Problem of Proof in Alfred de Musset's *Un Caprice* and *La Quenouille de Barbérine*', *Romance Notes*, 38: 1 (Fall 1997), 87–95.

Moser, Walter, 'Le Carnaval et le Cardinal', *Romantisme*, 19 (1978), 94–108.

Musset, Alfred de, *Œuvres complètes en prose*, éd. Maurice Allem (Paris Gallimard, 1951).

——, *Théâtre complet*, éd. Maurice Allem (Paris: Gallimard, 1952).

——, *Poésies complètes*, éd. Maurice Allem (Paris: Gallimard, 1957).

——, *Théâtre complet*, éd. Simon Jeune (Paris: Gallimard, 1990).

——, *Fantasio*, éd. Arnaud Tripet (Paris: Librairie Générale Française, 1993).

Nameri, Dorothey E., '*As You Like It/Fantasio*: a comparative study', in *Elizabethan Miscellany 2*, ed. James Hogg (Salzburg: Salzburg Studies in English Literature, 1978), 47–92.

Noe, Alfred, 'Les Débuts littéraires d'Alfred de Musset', *Cahiers du Centre d'Études des Tendances Marginales dans le Romantisme* Français, 4 (1994), 40–49.

Perrin-Naffakh, Anne-Marie, 'De la Convention à l'émotion: Le dialogue de Perdican et Rosette', *L'Information grammaticale,* vol. 49, 1991 March, 30–34.

Plata, Rajmunda, 'Le Temps et la liberté dans la parole de Lorenzo de Medicis', *Roczniki Humanistyczne*, 32: 5 (1984), 11–30.

Pommier, Jean, *Variétés sur Alfred de Musset et son théâtre* (Paris: Librairie Nizet, 1966).

Richard, Jean-Pierre. 'Arbres, herbes, fleurs: notes sur *Lorenzaccio*', *Rivista di letterature Moderne e Comparate*, 48: 4 (oct.–déc. 1995), 395–402.

Rickey, H. Wynn, *Musset Shakesperien* (Bourdeaux: Imprimerie de l'Académie et des Facultés, 1932).

Ruben, Vivien, 'The Idea of the Clown in Musset's *Fantasio*', *French Review*, 52: 5 (1979), 724–30.

Schor, Naomi, 'La Pèrodie: superpositions dans *Lorenzaccio*' in *Discours et pouvoir*, ed. Ross Chambers (Ann Arbor: University of Michigan, 1982), 73–86.

Sices, David, *Theater of Solitude: the drama of Alfred de Musset* (University Press of New England: Hanover, 1974).

Siegel, Patricia, *Alfred de Musset: a reference guide* (Boston: G.K. Hall, 982).

Simon, John K., 'The Presence of Musset in Modern French Drama', *French Review*, 40: 1 (1966), 27–38.

Smith, Albert, 'Musset's *Les Caprices de Marianne*: a romantic adaptation of a traditional comic structure', *Nineteenth-Century French Studies*, 20: 1–2 (Fall 1991–Winter 1992), 53–64.

St Ours, Kathryn, 'Le Conflit acte / pensée dans *Lorenzaccio*', *The French Review*, 67: 4 (mars 1994), 591–99.

Temkinde, Raymond, 'Musset sur scène aujourd'hui', *Europe* (nov.–déc. 1977), 40–59.

Thomas, Jean-Jacques, 'Les Maîtres-mots de Musset: peuple et pouvoir dans *Lorenzaccio*' in *Peuple et Pouvoir*, ed. Michel Glatigny (Lille: Presse Universitaire de Lille, 1981), 179–96.

Thomas, Merlin, 'Alfred de Musset: Don Juan on the Boulevard de Gand', in *Myth and its Making in the French Theatre, Studies presented to W.D. Howarth*, eds. E. Freeman, *et al.* (Cambridge: Cambridge University Press, 1988), 158–65.

Thomasseau, Jean-Marie, *Alfred de Musset:* Lorenzaccio (Paris: Presses Universitaires de France, 1986).

Tonge, Frederick, *L'Art du dialogue dans les comédies en prose d'Alfred de Musset* (Paris: Librairie A.G. Nizet, 1967).

Ubersfeld, Anne, 'Révolution et topique de la cité: *Lorenzaccio*', *Littérature*, 24 (déc. 1976), 40–50.

——, 'Le Portrait du peintre', *Revue des Sciences Humaines*, 42: 165 (jan.–mars 1977), 39–48.

——, 'Le Moi-statue', in *Journées d'études sur Alfred de Musset* (Clermont-Ferrand: Société des Études Romantiques, 1978), 63–79.

Villaneix, Paul, 'Musset et le Christ', *Revue de l'Histoire Littéraire de la France* (mars–avril 1976), 228–38.

Whitaker, M.-J., *Lorenzo ou Lorenzaccio: splendeurs et misères du héros romantique* (Paris: Lettres Modernes, 1989).

Musset Special Issues:

Europe: Alfred de Musset (nov.–déc. 1977).

Journées d'études sur Alfred de Musset (Clermont-Ferrand: Société des Études Romantiques, 1978).

Alfred de Vigny

Chotard, Loïc, 'Vigny lecteur de Corneille', *Revue d'Histoire Littéraire de la France*, 98: 3 (mai–juin 1998), 403–15.

Citoleux, Marc, *Alfred de Vigny: persistances classiques et affinités étrangères* (Paris: Champion, 1924).

Dale, R.C., '*Chatterton* is the Essential Romantic Drama, *L'Esprit Créateur*, 5: 3 (Fall 1965), 131–7.

Denommé, Robert T., '*Chatterton* ou le dilemme du héros dans un monde non-héroïque', *Cahiers de l'Association internationale des études françaises*, 35 (mai 1983), 141–54.

Drissa, Mohamed Ali, *Vigny et le symbole* (Tunis: Publications de l'Université de Tunis, 1979).

Jourdheuil, Jean, 'L'escalier de *Chatterton*', *Romantisme*, 38 (1982), 107–16.

Kushner, Eva, 'Histoire et théâtre chez Vigny', *L'Esprit Créateur*, 5: 3 (Fall 1965), 147–61.

Vigny, Alfred de, *Œuvres complètes* (Paris: Gallimard, 1986).

Vigny Special Issues:

Vigny: connu, méconnu, inconnu, Revue d'Histoire Littéraire de la France, 98: 3 (mai–juin 1998).

Cahiers de l'Association Internationale des études françaises, 45 (mai 1993).

Index

Abraham, Pierre 51n
Aristotle 10
Académie Française 129
Aeschylus 54
Allem, Maurice 83n
Balzac, Honoré de 4, 33n, 54n; *La Recherche de l'absolu* 33n
Bakhtine, Mikhail 70–71
Bandello 23
Barbéris, Pierre 51–52
Bataille, Georges 6, 12, 31, 46–47, 52, 56–64, 82, 90, 97–98; L'Érotisme 56–64, 90; 'Lascaux, ou la naissance de l'art ' 97–98; 'La notion de dépense 46–47
Bauman, Richard 7
Bem, Jeanne 99n
Bocage 25, 37
Bonaparte, Napoléon 9, 10, 12, 13, 53
Bonaparte, Napoléon III 53
Byron, Lord George 19

Carlson, Marvin 7n, 71
Carmontelle, Louis de 26
Chamber, Ross 111n
Charles X, king of France 9
Chatterton, Thomas 42
Chotard, Loïc 94n
Chaucer, Geoffrey, 'The Clerk's Tale' 15n
Le Conservateur Littéraire 53
Constant, Benjamin 11

Corneille, Pierre 128–9; *Querelle du Cid* 129
Crouzet, Michael 94

Delavigne, Casimir 64
Dessons, Gérard 26
Diderot, Denit, 11, 119n
Dorval, Marie 25, 37
Drury Lane Theatre, London 34
Ducis, Jean-François 69n
Dumas, Alexandre *père* 4, 11, 17, 19, 25, 31–42. 64–65. 127; *Antony* 17, 31, 36–43, 48, 49, 73, 75n, 121; *Le Comte de Monte-Cristo* 31; *Henri III et sa cour* 11, 31; *Kean ou désordre et génie* 17, 25, 31–37, 42, 48, 49, 73, 74, 121; *Richard Darlington* 31; *La Tour de Nesle* 31; *Les Trois Mousquetaires* 31
Durkheim, Émile 3
Duprez, Édouard 74
Durand, Régis 7n

Forte, Jeanie 7n
France, Revolution of 1789 9, 10, 12, 13, 51, 53
Frédérick-Lemaître 65

Gand, Eric 117–21
Gauthier, Théophile 54n
Germain, François 26n
Girard, René 52, 55, 63–64, 76, 82, 89

Goethe, Johann Wolfgang von 19

Hemmings, F.W.J. 31
Hoffman, E.T.A. 19
Howarth, W.D. 45n, 62
Hugo, Victor 4, 6, 9, 10, 19, 51–81, 101, 122n, 127; 'Preface de *Cromwell*' 10, 52–53; *Hernani* 9–12, 31, 53–64, 66, 73–79; *Lucrèce Borgia* 101n; *Marion de Lorme* 63n; *Le Roi s'amuse* 53, 54, 73–79; *Ruy Blas* 53, 54, 64–73, 75, 77–79, 122n

Jarry, André 26n
Jeune, Simon 83, 96n
Joly, Anténor 65
Jomarand, Jacqueline de 65n
July Monarchy, France 9

Kean, Edmund 31
Krakovitch, Odile 10n

Louis XVI, king of France 13, 26
Louis-Philippe, king of France 9

Maclean, Marie 100n
Malachy, Thérèse 100n
Malthus, Cecil 110–11
Marivaux, *L'Épreuve* 15n; *Le Jeu de l'amour et du hasard* 15n
Mars, Mlle 54
Marx, Karl 107–8
Masson, Bernard 106
Mauss, Marcel 21n
McCall, Dorothy 32
McCready, Susan 15n, 109n
Molière 10n, 128
Moser, Walter 103–4

Musset, Alfred de 4, 12, 13, 15n, 16–25, 26n, 27, 61n, 71, 81–128; *André del Sarto* 12n; *À quoi rêvent les jeunes filles* 36n; *Un Caprice* 2, 15, 16, 18–26, 48, 122n; *Les Caprices de Marianne* 81, 83–93, 99, 114; *Le Chandelier* 36n; *La Confession d'un enfant du siècle* 12–13, 17, 19; *La Coupe et les lèvres* 117; *Fantasio* 33n, 113–26, 128; *Il ne faut jurer de rien* 36n; 'Lettres de Dupuis et Cotonet' 19; *Lorenzaccio* 61n, 73, 75n, 81, 99–114, 116–21, 124, 125; *Les Marrons du feu* 117; *La Nuit Vénitienne* 18, 36n; *On ne Badine pas avec l'amour* 81, 92–99, 13, 114; *La Quenouille de Barbérine* 15n, 16, 18–26, 48; *Un Spectacle dans un fauteuil* 18
Musset, Paul de 114

Nerval, Gérard de 54n
Nietzsche 81

Odéon, Paris 12
Opéra, Paris 25

Pavis, Patrice 6
Perrault, Charles, 'Griselidis' 15n
Planche, Gustave 65
Przybos, Julia 3

Racine, Jean 128
Reinelt, Janelle G. 7n, 71n
Restoration 9, 10, 51
La Revue des deux mondes 18, 83, 92, 114

Rey, Pierre-Louis 40
Roach, Joseph R. 7n, 71n

Salyer, Jeffrey 6n
Sand, George 18, 96n
Sartre, Jean-Paul 31, 34n
Scarry, Elaine 8, 15–16, 22, 82, 85, 89, 93–94, 104, 107–8, 127; *The Body in Pain* 8, 15–16, 89, 107–8
Schechner, Richard 4, 5, 71
Schiller, J.C.F. von 19
Schopp, Claude 38n
Schor, Naomi 111
Scott, Walter 19
Shakespeare, William 19, 25, 31, 65, 75, 110–13; *Hamlet* 31, 110–13; *Othello* 12, 15n, 25, 31, 69n; *Romeo and Juliet* 31, 34; *A Winter's Tale* 15n
Sices, David 83, 118n
Staël, Germaine de 11
States, Bert O. 7
Steiner, George 65
Stendhal, *Racine et Shakespeare* 10, 129

Théâtre de la Comédie Française, Paris 9–12, 25, 42, 54, 63n, 64, 69, 83, 114, 128
Théâtre du Gymnase, Paris 26n
Théâtre Italien 74
Théâtre Lyrique, Paris 74
Théâtre de la Porte-Saint-Martin, Paris 37
Théâtre de la Renaissance, Paris 64–65
Théâtre des Variétés, Paris 31
Tripet, Arnaud 122
Turner, Victor 5, 52, 71

Ubersfeld, Anne 6, 10n, 16n, 32, 39, 53, 54, 63n, 65n, 70–71, 106n

Verdi, Giuseppe, *Rigoletto* 74
Vigny, Alfred de 4, 11–12, 17, 25–31, 36, 42–49, 127; *Chatterton* 2, 12, 17, 25, 33n, 36, 42–49, 73, 75n, 121, character of Kitty Bell in 2, 44–48; 'Dernière nuit de travail' 42; *Le More de Venise* 12, 25; *Poèmes antiques et modernes* 25, 46; *Quitte pour la peur* 17, 25–32, 36, 37, 48, 49; *Stello* 42
Voltaire 11, 28; *Zaïre* 28–29

Wright, Rachel 118n

Zola, Émile 4

EU authorised representative for GPSR:
Easy Access System Europe, Mustamäe tee 50,
10621 Tallinn, Estonia
gpsr.requests@easproject.com

www.ingramcontent.com/pod-product-compliance
Ingram Content Group UK Ltd.
Pitfield, Milton Keynes, MK11 3LW, UK
UKHW041121220326
4879IPUK00010B/6